Religious Education

Education

ages 7–11

TEACHING WITH text

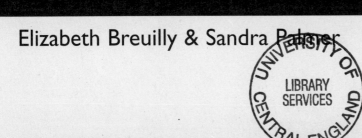

Elizabeth Breuilly & Sandra Palmer

Published by Scholastic Ltd,
Villiers House,
Clarendon Avenue,
Leamington Spa,
Warwickshire
CV32 5PR

Text © Elizabeth Breuilly and Sandra Palmer
© 2001
Scholastic Ltd
2 3 4 5 6 7 8 9 0   1 2 3 4 5 6 7 8 9 0

Authors
Elizabeth Breuilly and Sandra Palmer

Editor
Nancy Terry

Assistant Editor
Dulcie Booth

Series designer
Lynne Joesbury

Designer
Paul Cheshire

Illustrations
Beverly Curl

Cover illustration
Jon Berkeley

British Library Cataloguing-in-Publication Data
A catalogue record for this book is available from
the British Library.

ISBN 0-439-01784-X

Contents

Acknowledgements

Mariam Bassa for 'Going on Hajj' © 2001, Mariam Bassa, previously unpublished.

Martine Batchelor for 'The Life of a Zen Buddhist Nun' © 2001, Martine Batchelor, previously unpublished.

Elizabeth Breuilly for 'The Story of Geshe Ben' by Elizabeth Breuilly from the BBC Radio programme "Together" © 1997, Elizabeth Breuilly (1997, BBC Radio).

Elizabeth Breuilly and Sandra Palmer for the use of 'Susan's Diary' and 'A Letter from Mombasa' © 2001, Elizabeth Breuilly amd Sandra Palmer, previously unpublished.

Debjani Chatterjee for the use of 'Monkey Face' from *The Monkey God and other Hindu Tales* by Debjani Chatterjee © 1993, Debjani Chatterjee (1993, Rupa & Co.).

The Guardian for the use of extracts from 'Sunday Best' by Nigel Duckers from the *Guardian* Newspaper (8 Jan 2000) © 2000 The Guardian (2000, The Guardian Newspaper).

Kingsway's Thankyou Music for 'How Great Thou Art' by Stuart K. Hine from *Songs and Hymns of Fellowship* © 1953, Stuart K. Hine/S.K. Hine Trust (1953, Kingsway).

The Jewish Publication Society of America for 'Reb Meir Bear' by David Einhorn from *The Kid's Catalog of Jewish Holidays* by David A. Adler © 1996, David Einhorn (1996, The Jewish Publication Society) and 'Laws concerning the mezuzah' by Rabbi Hershel Matt and Stu Copans from *The First Jewish Catalog* by Richard Seigal, Michael and Sharon Strassfeld © 1973, Rabbi Hershel Matt and Stu Copans (1973, The Jewish Publication Society).

Jeremy Michelson for 'Interview with Jeremy Michelson' © 2001, Jeremy Michelson, previously unpublished.

Muslim Educational Trust for the use of extracts and illustrations on 'Wudu' from *Islam: Beliefs and Teachings* by Ghulam Sarwar © 1984, Muslim Educational Trust.

Abeda Patel for 'Why I agree with arranged marriages' © 2001, Abeda Patel, previously unpublished.

Ranchor Prime for 'Writing the Ramayana' by Ranchor Prime © 2001, Ranchor Prime, previously unpublished.

Reform Synagogues of Great Britain for the use of 'A selection of Jewish blessings' and Psalm 148: *A Hymn of Praise from Forms of Prayer for Jewish Worship Volume 1 Daily and Sabbath prayer book* © 1977, Reform Synagogues of Great Britain.

Shri Venkateswara (Balaji) Tividale, Oldbury, Birmingham for the use of information concerning their new Temple and Community Centre from their website © 1999, Shri Venkateswara (Balaji) Temple. (www.venkateswara.org.uk).

Transedition for the use of the extract 'Four Noble Truths' from *Religions of the World* by Elizabeth Breuilly, Joanne O'Brien and Martin Palmer © 1997, Elizabeth Breuilly et al (1997, Macdonald Young Books).

Introduction

The study of texts as part of religious education

The study of texts has a time-honoured, central place in the world's major religions. Jewish scholars pore over the scriptures, debating the interpretations of those who have gone before them; Buddhist monks study the canons of the Buddha's teaching, transmitted and written down over centuries; Muslim children learn Arabic after school so that they can learn to recite and then study the Qur'an; in Hindu thought, jnana (knowledge), which includes study of the scriptures, is one of the three ways of working towards release from rebirth. It can be argued that the drive towards universal literacy came from those Protestant reformers who wanted to make the Bible accessible to all.

The study of texts is also an important aspect of the work of those studying religious belief and practice, enabling students to gain an understanding of them. Texts are often the primary source material for such study, whether they be historical texts or contemporary writing. If RE is to be seen not just as the accumulation of a body of knowledge, but also as a means of developing thinking and reasoning skills in the context of religion, then religious literacy – the ability to interpret religious writings – cannot be ignored.

Learning to understand religious writings

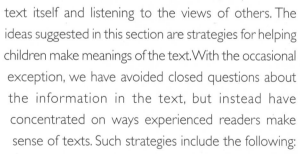

The starting point for understanding any text, whether religious or secular, from a sacred book, a book of carols, or an Internet text, has to be enabling children to engage with the text and to make a meaning of the text itself. Thus the primary objective for each text is that the children will engage with it and make meanings which are coherent with it. Since texts generate multiple meanings we cannot prescribe what these meanings will be, although some texts permit a narrower range of interpretation than others.

'Discussing the text' is a shorthand heading for sharing the text with the children, helping them engage with it, and making a response to it in the

light of their prior knowledge and personal experience. It refers to focusing on the text itself and listening to the views of others. The ideas suggested in this section are strategies for helping children make meanings of the text. With the occasional exception, we have avoided closed questions about the information in the text, but instead have concentrated on ways experienced readers make sense of texts. Such strategies include the following:

◆ Making an initial response to the text unguided by someone else's questions. This is particularly important in relation to a story, which is not read in the first instance as a source for information. In classroom practice the teacher simply asks the children to make a response in a very open way, for example, 'Say something about the story'.

◆ Using the title to guide reading.

◆ Bringing prior knowledge to the text.

◆ Skipping unknown words to gain a sense of the whole text; revisiting the word if it is essential to the context, by looking firstly for clues from the context and secondly in the dictionary.

◆ Wondering and talking about the text with someone else. We hope that the questions suggested will be viewed as a means of encouraging conversation, and modelling ways of questioning – scaffolding the children's learning rather than testing them for understanding.

◆ Being unconcerned about accurate pronunciation of unknown words, especially foreign ones. We recommend making intelligent guesses at words, based on looking at the syllables. You can then check pronunciation with any visiting speakers from the religion, or encourage children to check it should they have an opportunity.

◆ Forming mental images.

◆ Making headings and summaries.

◆ Using the text to inform another purpose (for example, composing a score to go with a script, or writing another information text, develops understanding of the script).

Understanding a text, however, is much more than making an initial meaning of it. Each time we read a text we may make fresh meaning, perhaps because we notice things we overlooked before, perhaps because we look at it from a different angle or perspective, or perhaps because we ourselves have changed. Sometimes subsequent readings are radically different from the first ones, sometimes the consequence is an enlarged meaning.

There are many ways in which our understanding of a text may be enlarged beyond an initial interpretation of words on a page. These include:

◆ Recognizing whether the text is written by an author from within the religion, or from outside it.

◆ Knowledge of how the text, particularly one from a sacred book, is interpreted by people within the religion. That is not to say children are obliged to share that interpretation as though there were one definitive meaning of the text; even within the faith there may be controversy over how the text is to be interpreted.

◆ Knowledge of the historical context in which the text was written.

◆ Knowledge of how the text relates to the beliefs and practices of the religion which generated it.

Suggestions on how to develop the children's understanding of the wider context can be found mainly under the 'Further RE activities' section. Suggestions are also given here for discussions which move away from the text but are stimulated by the themes and issues provoked by the text. The text may provide a perspective on the issue.

Teaching with texts as part of an RE unit or scheme of work

Although we give some quite detailed guidance on how to enable children to make meaning of the text, the teachers' notes are not lesson plans, and the texts are not presented as units of work. They are intended for flexible use in the classroom. Some could be used as a starting point, the foundation on which a unit of work is constructed. All can be used as part of a unit of work, complementing other teaching strategies. An approach to RE which concentrated only on interpreting texts could become very dry. We have indicated in the teachers' notes where prior knowledge is needed to make sense of the text.

The choice and breadth of texts

This collection of texts from different religions reflects some of the diversity of genre in religious writings. They have been chosen or commissioned because the topics they touch are part and parcel of the general practice of religious education in the junior school. We have included texts from the scriptures so that children can have direct access to some sacred writings, texts written from an encounter with a faith, and very personal texts which give the writer's perspective and experience of their religion, but which should not be taken as in any way 'representative' or 'typical'.

They include some stories which are clearly didactic. These have developed in the religion to illustrate a belief or make a moral point. Acknowledging that they were written for this purpose is part of understanding the text.

There are some stories which bear the hallmark of legend – stories which are set in historical times, and perhaps had historical roots, but have been embellished with heroic or magical detail. Others are more mythological – tales whose supernatural element is so strong that it is apparent that their claim to truth lies in what is said about human nature, rather than by reference to historical events.

The very nature of myth and legend, handed down from generation to generation via oral tradition, means that we cannot know their original authors; what we have instead are versions by particular authors and collectors. The long oral tradition behind such texts may also result in a number of versions being in circulation; the basic plot is the same but the detail differs.

Few of these are texts which one would expect the majority of junior children to read on their own. They are texts for shared reading, using some of the strategies drawn from the National Literacy Strategy. Shared reading enables children to approach more challenging texts, ones that they might not be able to read by themselves or which have too much in them to comprehend purely by listening. It gives them access to religiously interesting material; it develops their reading skills in the context of RE (see above) and broadens their religious vocabulary.

Teaching with texts and the National Literacy Strategy

The texts reflect some of the diversity of genre to be found in the National Literacy Strategy, and it may be that you will wish to incorporate them within your literacy programme. With all the pressures on the curriculum, overlapping RE and literacy makes good economic use of time. More importantly, it is difficult to disentangle RE from language and literacy since so much RE work involves speaking, listening, writing and comprehension of texts. We have made suggestions for further language work which moves away from RE at the end of each section of the teachers' notes. However, the primary focus of this book is religious education, and it is written with those aims and objectives in mind.

Finally

We encourage you to approach these texts with a spirit of adventure. Do not be afraid of exploring with the children a text that you may not fully understand yourself. Few people within any given religion would claim to understand fully the texts which are important to them. Do not be afraid, also, to engage with the emotions of religion: read the stories, poems and personal accounts in as dramatic a way as possible, and encourage the children to 'enter into' each text in their imagination. This is not the same as inviting belief, but enables a freer exploration of belief, which is the essential aim and purpose of this book.

Buddhism

EXTRACT	GENRE	RE OBJECTIVES	LITERACY LEARNING OBJECTIVES	PAGE
The Four Noble Truths	Information text/rules, plans, etc.	◆ To develop understanding of Buddhism and its central teaching on suffering.	◆ To gain information from lists and formulae. ◆ To use story to illustrate a moral.	12
The Story of Geshe Ben	Traditional story from a range of cultures – Tibetan Buddhism	◆ To develop understanding of one aspect of the Eightfold Path. ◆ To discuss stealing.	◆ To follow narrative and speech in a story. ◆ To encounter a traditional tale.	16
Kisagotami and the Mustard Seed	Traditional story/narrative poem	◆ To interpret stories of the Buddha. ◆ To know the Buddhist teaching about suffering and death. ◆ To provide an opportunity to talk about feelings.	◆ To understand narrative poetry. ◆ To understand mood in poetry. ◆ To understand metaphor in poetry.	22
While Peace Reigns	Traditional story/story from another culture	◆ To develop familiarity with a Buddhist way of telling legends. ◆ To discuss co-operation and working together.	◆ To discuss features of traditional stories. ◆ To discuss didactic stories.	26
Memories of a Buddhist Childhood	Non-fiction/autobiography	◆ To highlight the practice of the Buddhist faith.	◆ To identify features of personal memoir. ◆ To look at ways of expressing habitual action.	30
The Life of a Zen Buddhist Nun	Non-fiction/autobiography	◆ To learn about the life of a Buddhist monk or nun. ◆ To consider the benefits of reflection.	◆ To identify features of personal memoir. ◆ To look at ways of expressing habitual action.	34

Christianity

EXTRACT	GENRE	RE OBJECTIVES	LITERACY LEARNING OBJECTIVES	PAGE
A Hymn to Love	Poetry	◆ To develop an understanding of the Christian concept of love.	◆ To understand personification of an abstract quality.	41
How Great Thou Art	Poetry/hymns	◆ To develop the idea that praise is important in Christian worship. ◆ To look at the concept of God creating the world.	◆ To understand archaic forms of English used in verse. ◆ To appreciate mood in poetry.	44
Susan's Diary	Non-fiction/personal writing, diary	◆ To develop knowledge of the Christian rite of baptism. ◆ To look at how we show commitment.	◆ To discuss the practice and format of keeping a diary. ◆ To read colloquial language.	47
Prayers from the Celtic Tradition	Poetry/including prayer and poetry from different places and times	◆ To develop familiarity with the range of prayers. ◆ To learn some reasons why people pray.	◆ To understand what is an oral tradition. ◆ To understand archaic language. ◆ To appreciate rhythm and repetition in poetry	50
The Pilgrim's Hymn	Poetry/hymn	◆ To develop familiarity with a major Christian hymn. ◆ To allow an opportunity to think about life as a pilgrimage. ◆ To reflect on doing your best.	◆ To begin to identify features of earlier periods in poetry. ◆ To encounter the vocabulary of mythical beings. ◆ To understand symbolism and allegory.	55
John Bunyan	Non-fiction/biography	◆ To learn about a well-known Christian figure. ◆ To look at standing up for your beliefs.	◆ To glean information from a factual account. ◆ To understand a biographical account.	58
Christmas Bells (Longfellow's Carol)	Poem in ballad form/carol	◆ To develop an understanding of the Christmas message of peace and goodwill.	◆ To understand a message in poetic form. ◆ To relate the message of a poem to information about the writer.	62
A Legend of the Wise Men	Fiction/legend	◆ To develop awareness of the legends of Christianity. ◆ To provide opportunity for discussion on prejudice.	◆ To appreciate the characteristics of legend. ◆ To explore metaphor.	66

Hinduism

EXTRACT	GENRE	RE OBJECTIVES	LITERACY LEARNING OBJECTIVES	PAGE
A Letter from Mombasa	Non-fiction account of events	◆ To develop understanding of Hindu places of worship. ◆ To reflect on ways of showing respect in religious buildings.	◆ To look at letter-writing style. ◆ To glean information from a non-fiction source.	73
Monkey Face	Fiction/traditional tale	◆ To widen familiarity with the tradition of Hindu storytelling. ◆ To reflect on pride and vanity.	◆ To look at features of traditional tales.	78
Writing the Ramayana	Journal or personal writing with reference to myth	◆ To extend understanding of the Hindu epic – the Ramayana, by seeing how one person has responded to it.	◆ To understand and develop personal response to texts.	83
Tividale Tirumala A Dream in the Making	Information – public information from the Internet	◆ To learn about a Hindu Temple in Britain.	◆ To glean information from public information and Internet sources. ◆ To use dictionaries and reference books to help understand a text. ◆ To pick up textual clues about target audience	89

Buddhism

Buddhism began in India in the 6th century BC with the teachings of Siddhartha Gautama, later known as the Buddha or 'enlightened one'. It then spread east through Tibet and China. There is a vast amount of traditional Buddhist scripture, in a variety of languages. For several centuries the early teachings of the Buddha were passed down orally by the community of Buddhist monks and nuns. They were recorded in written form in Sri Lanka in the first century BC, in Pali, an Indian language probably close to that which the Buddha himself spoke. This collection is known as the Pali Canon. The Northern (Mahayana) tradition of Buddhism has scriptures in Sanskrit, Tibetan and Chinese. Some of these various texts are held to be the words of the Buddha himself, others are commentaries and further reflections by scholars and sages. Very little of this material is at a level suitable for children but we have included the core teachings as a text.

In addition, there are many traditional tales about the life of the Buddha. The story of 'Kisagotami and the Mustard Seed' is one such story, movingly told in poetic form. There are also many popular legends and traditional tales, some based on the belief that the Buddha is an eternal figure with many lives and incarnations. Wise teachers and self-sacrificing heroic figures in whatever form, from the hare to the monkey, are seen as incarnations of the Buddha, and foolish characters are foolish disciples who had much difficulty learning and caused suffering to others in their thoughtlessness. The story 'While Peace Reigns' is from this genre, known as the Jataka Tales.

Another story tells of one of the Buddha's later followers, Geshe Ben, illustrating Buddhist teachings but also embodying a recurring theme in religion, that of repentance and the struggle with the 'weaker' self.

Two other texts are modern, personal ones, about being a Buddhist engaging with the beliefs today. One is an account from a young woman, raised as a Buddhist, about her understanding of her faith. The other is by a Buddhist nun, a convert, writing about life in the monastery.

The Four Noble Truths

Genre

information text: rules/ plans

The Buddha taught these in his first sermon at Sarnath. He told his disciples that to understand the Four Noble Truths, the mind must first be at peace:

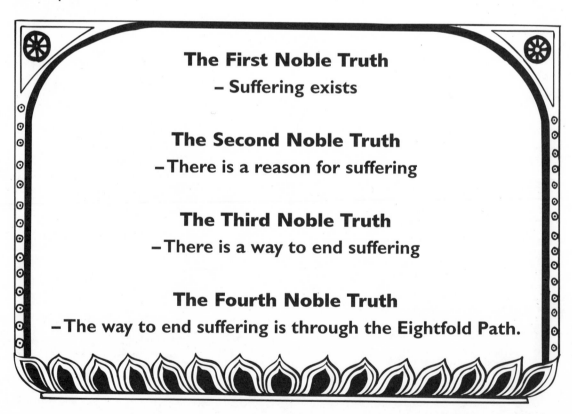

The First Noble Truth

– Suffering exists

The Second Noble Truth

– There is a reason for suffering

The Third Noble Truth

– There is a way to end suffering

The Fourth Noble Truth

– The way to end suffering is through the Eightfold Path.

From Religions of the World (Macdonald Young Books, 1997),
by Elizabeth Breuilly, Joanne O'Brien and Martin Palmer

The Eightfold Path

The Buddha's path to end suffering involves discipline of both thought and action. In order to follow it, many Buddhists find a teacher to guide them, and once they have listened and understood the meaning of the Eightfold Path, they try to practise it.

1. **Right Views** – knowing and understanding the Four Noble Truths

2. **Right Thoughts** – letting go of want and desire, and acting with kindness to avoid hurting anything

3. **Right Speech** – telling the truth, speaking kindly and wisely

4. **Right Action** – not stealing or cheating

5. **Right Livelihood** – earning a living that does not cause bloodshed or harm to others

6. **Right Effort** – encouraging and developing positive thought in order to keep to the Path

7. **Right Mindfulness** – being aware of thoughts and actions that affect the world now and in the future

8. **Right Concentration** – this is the peaceful state of mind which arises through correct practice of the Eightfold Path.

The Four Noble Truths

Genre
information text: rules/ plans

RE objective

◆ To develop understanding of the central teachings of Buddhism.

Previous knowledge

The story of the Buddha's search for enlightenment would be useful.

Background notes

This text sets out the heart of Buddhist teaching, summarizing the Buddha's first sermon after he experienced enlightenment. It might be used in the context of a unit of work on Buddhism in which the children have first heard about the life of the Buddha Siddhartha Gautama. According to tradition, Siddhartha Gautama reached enlightenment at Bodh Gaya, and preached his first sermon to a few disciples at Sarnath shortly afterwards.

Key words

Noble; suffering; eightfold.

Discussing the text

◆ Put the text in the context of the life of the Buddha, which they have already heard. Ask the children to recall that the search started with the problem of suffering and how to end it. Look at the title and the opening sentence. Have a general discussion about the meanings of the words 'noble' and 'truths'. What do the children expect the passage to be about?

◆ Look at the sentence which sets the scene. Check the children know the meaning of the words 'sermon' and 'disciple'. Ask them to imagine the scene.

◆ Then look at the layout of the rest of the page. Is this the sermon itself or a summary of the teachings in the sermon?

◆ Take the first Noble Truth. Ask the children to recall the suffering that the Buddha himself witnessed (old age, sickness, death, and religious asceticism). Prompt them to suggest examples of suffering in the contemporary world.

◆ Read the next three Noble Truths, and then ask the children whether these truths could be set out in a different order.

◆ Finally, read the Eightfold Path, noting the repetition of the word 'right'. Discuss with the children the metaphor of a path (for example, why a 'path' rather than a 'plan' or a 'system' or 'rules'?). What images do they have of a path? What images would someone who lived in a mountainous region have of a path?

◆ Suggest the children draw a picture for each aspect of the path. This could be a symbol, or a picture of someone doing something.

◆ Ask the children to identify which sections are about thinking and attitudes, and which are about actions.

◆ Discuss how the Eightfold Path and the Four Noble Truths are linked. Let the children express their own ideas of how following the path might reduce suffering or help people to live with suffering.

Further RE activities

◆ Learn more about Buddhist monks and nuns and how they try to follow this path (see 'The Life of a Zen Buddhist Nun', page 34).

◆ Read a story or fable from Buddhism which illustrates one or more aspects of the path. 'The Story of Geshe Ben' (page 16) is one example, illustrating 'right livelihood'. 'While Peace Reigns' (page 26) could be discussed as an example of 'right speech' (and its opposite!). 'Right thoughts' are illustrated by 'The Hare Mark on the Moon' and 'The Monkey Bridge' in *A Tapestry of Tales* (see the Resources list, page 160).

◆ Discuss the link between bad thoughts and bad actions. Does one necessarily lead to the other?

◆ Pick up further the link between the Eightfold Path and suffering, and discuss each aspect in more depth.

◆ Children draw a picture for each aspect of the path. This could be a symbol, or a picture of someone doing something.

Further literacy ideas

◆ Look at the use of capital letters in the text to signify titles or something important.

◆ Note that, like many explanatory texts, it is not written entirely in sentences and that there are no paragraphs.

◆ Note the use of numerals in the Eightfold Path, and the use of words for numbers in the Four Noble Truths. Why might the authors have done this?

◆ Children write their own moral tale of how having bad or greedy thoughts led someone to wrong actions.

The Story of Geshe Ben

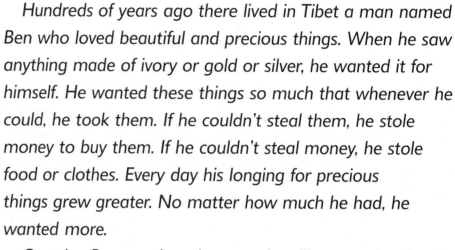

Genre
traditional
story from a
range of
cultures:
Tibetan
Buddhism

1. Hundreds of years ago there lived in Tibet a man named Ben who loved beautiful and precious things. When he saw anything made of ivory or gold or silver, he wanted it for himself. He wanted these things so much that whenever he could, he took them. If he couldn't steal them, he stole money to buy them. If he couldn't steal money, he stole food or clothes. Every day his longing for precious things grew greater. No matter how much he had, he wanted more.

2. One day Ben was hanging round a village market, but he felt that someone was watching him. It was a Buddhist monk who sat very still and quiet, and seemed to take no notice of what was going on around him, but his eyes were open and Ben didn't dare steal anything.

3. Then he thought, "That monk has been here since early morning, he's had nothing to eat, and now it's almost midday. Maybe if he has some food, he'll go away."

4. Ben sat down beside the monk.

5. "Here," he said. "Have some of my rice."

6. "Thank you," said the monk. "Your kindness will have its reward. The Buddha teaches us that everything we do, both good and bad, brings its own result. Those who do bad things to others will suffer for it, either in this life or in a life to come. Those who are kind will find that others are kind to them. But oh, you poor man, how tightly you are bound by that strong rope!"

7. "What on earth do you mean?" said Ben. "What rope? I am not tied up."

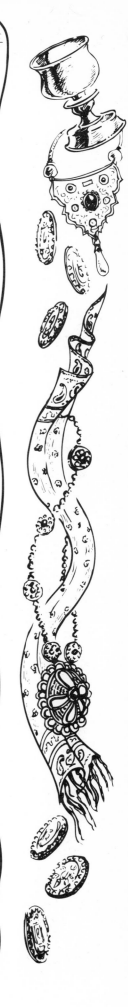

8.   *"You may not feel it now," replied the monk, "but there is a rope made up of everything you have ever done and everything you have ever thought, which is binding you to life after life of pain and suffering. Do you see that dog?"*

9.   *Between two houses, a dog was tied to a tree on a long rope. It was quite happy running about, but it was slowly winding the rope round and round the tree.*

10.   *"That dog thinks he is free. But in the end, he will find that he can only go round and round, and the rope will bind him ever closer to the tree. People who chase after what they want without thinking of others are like that dog. They are tied by their own actions and thoughts. When they die, they will not be free, for they will be reborn, to run round and round the same tree again and again, in life after life.*

11.   *"I watched you as you saw the people with their silver coins. I watched your eyes when a rich man walked past dressed in silk robes. You love these things, you want them, you are tied to them just as the dog is tied to the tree. You think they will make you happy, but you always want more, and the misery you cause to other people will eventually make your life miserable."*

12.   *Ben sat very still. He thought about the silver coins, and the silk robes of the rich man, and he felt the tugging and struggling inside himself that said, "I want it, I want it, I want it!"*

13.   *"You're right," he said. "I am bound hand and foot because I can't stop wanting things, and the people I steal from hate me. What shall I do? How can I escape?"*

14.   *"The way to release is simple," said the monk, "but it is not easy. The Lord Buddha taught us about a way to live our lives that eventually leads to calm, and peacefulness, and a release from endless lives. He called it the Eightfold Path because there are eight things to learn."*

15. "How can I find this path? How can I begin to follow it?" asked Ben.

16. "You have already begun, for you have seen and understood that stealing things will only make you unhappy. You have much to learn, but are you willing to follow in the footsteps of the Buddha?"

17. "I will do it! I will become a monk like you. I will give up stealing things, and I will read the words of the Buddha and think about them until they become my own thoughts."

18. So Ben went to live in a monastery high up in the Tibetan mountains. He lived on what people freely gave the monks out of the kindness of their hearts. Day after day he read what the Buddha taught and thought deeply about it, sitting quite still, his only movement a slow and gentle breathing in and breathing out. Day by day he felt calmer, happier, and more peaceful.

19. But although Ben was really sorry for stealing things, it wasn't easy to stop. One day a rich man came to visit the monastery, and among his belongings was a cup made of gold. It was quite small, but it was beautifully moulded and polished, and it gleamed in the lamplight. Ben looked at it.

20. "It's so lovely," he thought. "How I would love to have it, to feel its smooth surface, to see it shining in the sun... I would only borrow it."

21. As these thoughts went through his head, his right hand was slowly reaching out to the cup. Almost without knowing it, he took a step closer, his hand began to grasp the cup...

22. "Stop, thief!"

23. The quiet of the monastery was shattered, and the startled monks came running from all directions. There was Ben gasping and struggling, clutching his right hand, pulling it away from the precious cup.

24. "Who? Where? Which way did he go?" they cried.

25. "Calm yourselves," replied Ben. "The thief is here – my own right hand. It was I who shouted out to you to help me stop the theft, and with my left hand I pulled the villain back from taking anything. But alas! The thought was so strong in my mind! If my right hand had done what it thought of doing, it would not only have stolen a cup from our guest, it would have robbed me of all the steps I have taken towards peace of mind and happiness. Help me, my friends, help me!"

26. And so it became known in the monastery that if Ben cried out, or grabbed his right hand with his left, that meant he was fighting against his old habits. Again and again he found himself wanting to take some beautiful or precious thing that he saw, to have it and hold it and make it his. Then his friends would gather round and help him grow calm again, to let the wanting die down like a fire going out.

27. As he learned, he taught other people and tried to guide them in the footsteps of the Buddha, along the Eightfold Path, just as the monk had guided him. He became known as a wise and learned teacher, and as a good and kindly man. People gave him the highly honoured name of 'Geshe', which means 'Teacher'.

28. Did Geshe Ben ever reach the end of the path? We don't know for sure, and for many years he still heard the voice inside himself that said, "I want it, I want it, I want it!" But the voice grew fainter and fainter, and the echoes slowly died away. People from Tibet tell many stories of his later life, of how wise and calm he was, how he helped other people, and of how he no longer even dreamed of taking anything that was not freely given to him.

A Tibetan Buddhist story retold by Elizabeth Breuilly.

The Story of Geshe Ben

Genre
traditional story from a range of cultures: Tibetan Buddhism

RE objectives

◆ To develop understanding of one aspect of the Eightfold Path.

◆ To discuss stealing.

Previous knowledge

Although this story could stand on its own, it is best studied with some prior knowledge of Buddhism.

Background notes

As with many religious stories, this story from Tibetan Buddhism is difficult to categorize as either fiction or non-fiction. It is, rather, a traditional story which has a ring of truth about it. Geshe Ben may well have been a real living teacher, but no doubt his story is told to convey Buddhist teachings about stealing and compulsive behaviour, and the possibility of turning aside from such behaviour and changing. The prohibition against stealing is the fourth part of the Eightfold Path of Buddhism – the path the Buddha told his disciples to follow to avoid and alleviate suffering in the world.

The story falls into two episodes, perhaps best discussed in this way.

Key words

Eightfold Path; monastery; Lord Buddha.

Discussing the text

◆ Look at the title and the source. From which religion does the story come? What do the children recall about the religion? You may need to check that the children know what a monk is before you start.

◆ Read the first paragraph. What do we learn about Ben?

◆ Look at the first episode in paragraph 2–17. Read the conversation with the Buddhist monk, perhaps by dividing the class into three for each character and the narrator. Check the children's grasp of the plot and wonder about the text with them. Begin with an open question for a reaction to this episode.

◆ Draw a thought bubble for Ben and ask the children to suggest what he is thinking.

◆ Draw a thought bubble for the monk and again ask the children to suggest what he is thinking.

◆ Ask: 'In what ways is Ben like the dog running round in circles?'

◆ Ask: 'What do we learn about Buddhist teaching?'

◆ Discuss why the children think Ben wanted to become a monk. What do they think he would be like as a monk?

◆ Look at the second episode, perhaps as a second reading (in which case you will need to ask the children to recall what happened in the first one). Read paragraph 18 to the end. Quickly check the children's grasp of facts by asking: 'What did Ben do next?', 'Where did he go to live?', 'What did he do there?' and ask for an open response. Ask: 'Did Ben find it easy to give up his desire to steal?', 'How did he stop himself from stealing?', 'What reputation did Ben have when he was an old man?'

◆ Look back at the title. When and why does Ben become Geshe Ben? (See paragraph 27.)

◆ At the end of the session, invite the children to reflect on the passage. Tell them that this is an old story, hundreds of years old. Why do they think that people continue to tell the story of Geshe Ben today? Is there anything that people today can learn from his life? How do we learn from other people? Why does stealing cause suffering?

◆ What is addictive or compulsive behaviour? It wasn't easy for Geshe Ben to stop his stealing. How did he help himself? What can be learned from him?

Further RE activities

◆ Topics for further research by children:

– The life of the Buddha, the great teacher.

– The Eightfold Path. Children write modern-day examples.

– Life in a Buddhist monastery.

– Buddhist beliefs about reincarnation.

Further literacy ideas

◆ Children turn the dialogue in the market scene into speech and thought bubbles. Look at the alternating use of passages of dialogue and passages of narration in the text.

◆ Look at the beginning ('hundreds of years ago') and ending of the story (summing up the reaction to Ben's life at the end), both characteristic of traditional tales about noble teachers and saints.

Key words extension

◆ Make a glossary of other words associated with religious professions (for instance, nun, priest, rabbi, imam, bishop, abbot). Which words are particular to one faith only, which to more?

◆ Make a list of metaphors and similes in the story, and look at how they are used. (Note: the 'rope of desire', the similarity to the dog, desires dying down like a fire, are part of the Buddha's traditional teaching.)

◆ Ask the children to name and recall stories about other religious teachers, for example, Jesus and Mahatma Gandhi.

Kisagotami and the Mustard Seed

Genre
traditional
story;
narrative
poem

A woman dove-eyed, young, with tearful face
And lifted hands, greeted the Buddha; bending low she said,

"Lord, remember me. Yesterday I came to you, seeking help.
My child, my only child, straying amid some blossoms, found a snake.
It twined itself around his wrist, and my child laughed
And teased the quick-forked tongue.
Of that cold playmate.

But, alas! ere long
He turned so pale and still, I could not think
Why he should cease to play. And someone said, 'He is sick
Of poison,' and another, 'He will die.'

But I – I could not lose my precious boy,
I asked them for some cure which might bring the light
Back to my child's eyes.
That kiss-mark of the serpent was so very small, surely it could not
hurt him!

And someone said, 'There is a holy man upon the hill –
Look, he is passing now in his yellow robe. Ask him if there is a cure
for your child.'

And so I came to you, trembling, praying you to tell me what would
heal my child.
You did not spurn me but looked on me
with gentle eyes and touched me with a patient hand,
And you said to me,
'Yes, little sister, there is something that might heal
you first and him, if you could fetch the thing:

You must find a black mustard seed,
Only remember this one thing:
Do not take the seed from any hand or house
Where a father, mother, child or slave has died,
It shall be well if you can find such seed.'"

Kisagotami paused and silent stood.

The Buddha smiled,
Exceedingly tenderly. "Yes, I spoke like this
Dear Kisagotami. But did you find the seed?"

Kisagotami answered,

"I went, Lord, clasping to me
The babe grown colder. I asked at each hut –
Here in the jungle and towards the town –
'I pray you, give me mustard, a seed – a black one'
and each who had it, gave it
Since all the poor have pity on the poor.
But when I asked at the first home, 'In this household here, has anyone
died –
A husband or wife or child or slave?' they said,
'O Sister, what is this you ask? The dead
Are very many, and the living few!'
So with sad thanks I gave the mustard seed back.
And others said, 'Here is the seed, but we have lost our slave!'
'Here is the seed, but our good man is dead!'
'Here is some seed, but he that sowed it died
Between the rain time and the harvesting!'

Ah, sir! I could not find a single house
Where there was mustard seed and none had died!
Ah, sir! I could not find a single house.
Please tell me sir, where can I find this seed and not find death."

"My Sister! I would pour out my blood if I could stop the curse
that makes us grieve.
When you came yesterday your child was gone.
But now you know that
The whole world weeps with your woe.

Your child is dead; bury him."

Adapted from The Light of Asia by Sir Edwin Arnold. Quoted from Kerry Brown and Joanne O'Brien
(eds.) from The Essential Teachings of Buddhism (Rider, 1989)

Kisagotami and the Mustard Seed

Genre
traditional story; narrative poem

RE objectives

◆ To interpret stories of the Buddha.

◆ To know the Buddhist teaching about suffering and death.

◆ To provide an opportunity to talk about feelings.

Previous knowledge

A basic knowledge of who the Buddha was would be useful.

Background notes

The story of Kisagotami is one of the most deeply moving episodes in the life of the Buddha and is a lesson to all humanity. It is a story heard in all Buddhist lands and often beyond. We offer it to you in this version by Sir Edwin Arnold in his epic *The Light of Asia*, slightly adapted, rather than one retold for children since the poetic use of language adds to the pathos of the story. It is not an easy text but one which can be made accessible to children via the shared reading process. The problem of suffering is one that lies at the heart of Buddhism; it was the presence of suffering in the world which spurred the young Gautama to leave his life of luxury in the palace to seek the meaning of life.

The time sequence of the story is not easy to grasp immediately. Kisagotami recounts past events and past conversations within her speech, using direct rather than indirect speech to quote what has been said to her. The Buddha then responds to what has happened. Different fonts have been used to help make clear who is speaking in each instance. Try to read the poem with different voices depending on who is speaking: either assigning parts like a play, or using different voices yourself.

This is a story for wondering about with the children (see the Introduction, page 6), both at the language used and the theme of grief and death within it. It therefore invites a mellow, reflective manner when working with it. We suggest that the more difficult words are explained or skipped over rather than investigated immediately with a dictionary. It is clearly a story which demands sensitive handling.

Key words

Lord Buddha; grieve; woe.

Discussing the text

◆ Before reading the passage, look at the title and the layout of the text – what does it tell the reader? (For example, that it is about someone who is foreign, that it is a poem, and that it implies that something happens.)

◆ Ask the children to suggest how to pronounce 'Kisagotami', and decide jointly how you will pronounce it.

◆ Ask the children to look at the poem and see how many different people are speaking.

◆ First reading: read the first two lines and ask the children to make a mental image of it. Why does it feel like a sad poem from the start?

◆ Read the next stanza with the children. They may need help in understanding that the young woman is Kisagotami and she is reminding the Buddha of what happened yesterday. Why did she seek the Buddha's help? What had happened to her child? Who is the 'cold playmate'?

◆ Look at the next two stanzas. What happens in them? What does Kisagotami hope the Buddha will do?

◆ Kisagotami tells us how the Buddha behaved towards her. What did he tell her to do?

◆ Pause with the narrative and give a summary overview, and wonder rhetorically with the children about what will happen next.

◆ Read the next stanzas. Ask the children whether Kisagotami found a mustard seed. Why not?

◆ Read the Buddha's final speech. Why do they think that the Buddha did not tell her immediately when she first came to him that the child was already dead? What does Kisagotami know at the end of the poem that she didn't know when her child first died?

◆ Judge the mood of the children. If they seem ready, begin an open-ended discussion about the poem (see page 5 of the Introduction). If not, read the whole poem again, and hold the discussion then. You might mark the text with the children, using different underlining or colours, so that it is easy to read with different voices, including those of the villagers. Choose children to read the different parts, reminding them to try to convey some feeling as they read.

◆ Discuss with them how they would illustrate the story. What colours would they use? Why? Do they imagine the day being bright and sunny, or wet and moist and misty? Why?

◆ Second reading: remind the children of the poem and ask them to recall their feelings. Read the poem again and ask for other thoughts. Work with the children to write simple mood music for the poem using percussion, illustrating, for example, the child playing, the child becoming ill, Kisagotami's desperation and frantic search for a cure, her approach to the Buddha, her search for the mustard seed, and her realization that the child is dead.

Further RE activities

◆ Read other stories about the Buddha from this book and from other sources (see the Resources list, page 160).

◆ Read the summary of the Buddha's teaching found in the tale of the Four Noble Truths and the Eightfold Path (see page 12).

◆ Allow the children to reflect on and discuss their own feelings and experiences about death.

Further literacy ideas

◆ Pick out the words which convey the mood of the poem; it is not just the 'facts' of the story which make it sad. Ask the children to think of other words used to convey feelings.

◆ Discuss the metaphor of 'dove-eyed'. What sort of eyes are dove-eyed? Children discuss what images they have of the character or feelings of people who are described with other animal metaphors for eyes, for example, doe-eyed, cow-eyed, crocodile-eyed, tiger-eyed and snake-eyed. What other words can be used to describe eyes, other than colour?

◆ Discuss with the children why it is called a poem rather than just a story.

◆ Ask the children to rewrite the story as a straightforward narrative account.

◆ Rewrite the story as a play with several scenes, for example, Scene 1: the child playing, the snake bite, the child becoming ill, the neighbours offering advice; Scene 2: Kisagotami approaching the Buddha; Scene 3: the search for the mustard seed, and so on.

◆ Suggest the children recount a sad incident, perhaps something that happened to them, conscious of the vocabulary that draws out the sadness.

While Peace Reigns

Genre
*traditional
story; story
from another
culture*

This story was told by the Buddha while he was living in the Banyan-grove near Kapilavatthu. One of his followers accidentally pushed another and got his clothes dirty. Although he said sorry, the other would not accept it, and they each began to squabble and argue and call each other names. Their friends each took sides, and before long it seemed that everyone was bickering.

The Master, the Buddha, said to them, "Come, my friends. We are one family, we should not quarrel amongst ourselves! But this isn't the first time that the strength of peace and friendship was defeated by quarrelling." They asked him what he meant, and he told them this story:

Many lifetimes ago, there lived in the forest a huge flock of birds, who had a very wise and good leader. A hunter also lived in that forest; he made his living by catching birds and selling them for food. He used to imitate the sound of a bird so that they gathered together in one place, then he flung his net over them, and whipped the sides of the net together so as to get them all huddled up in a heap. Then he crammed them into his basket, and went home and sold them.

Now, one day the leader said to the birds, "This hunter is causing terrible losses in our tribe. I have a plan to stop him catching us. Next time he throws the net over us, each one of us must quickly stick his head through the mesh and fly up in the air as fast as we can. Then we'll fly to a thorny bush so that the net will be caught on the thorns, and we can each escape from underneath."

"Very good," they all eagerly agreed.

The next day, when the hunter threw his net over them, they did just as their leader had told them – they lifted up the net and let it down on a thorn-bush, and escaped from underneath. While the hunter was still trying to pick his net off the thorns, evening came on and he went away empty-handed. The next day and the next the birds played the same trick, and day after day the hunter was busy till sunset disentangling his net, and then had to go home empty-handed. As this went on, his wife grew angry and said, "Day by day you return empty-handed; I think you're cheating me!"

"No, my dear," said the hunter. "I'm not cheating you. The fact is those birds have begun to work together now. The moment my net is over them, off they fly with it and escape, leaving it on a thorn-bush. Still, they won't be able to go on working together for long. Don't you fret; as soon as they start bickering among themselves, I shall bag the lot, and that will bring a smile to your face. Just wait and see."

Not long after this, as the birds landed on their feeding ground, one of them trod by accident on another's head.

"Who trod on my head?" screeched the bruised bird.

"I did; but I didn't mean to. Don't be angry," said the first bird.

But the other wouldn't listen, and was still furious. That made the first bird angry, and they began to call each other names and argue, saying things like, "I suppose you think you lift up the net all by yourself? Well, just wait and see if you can manage without me!"

When he heard this, the birds' leader thought to himself, "If they're going to quarrel like this, we are all in danger. The time has come when they will no longer lift up the net, and they will all be destroyed. The hunter will get his chance. I can stay here no longer." So he gathered together a few faithful followers, and they flew away to another part of the forest.

Sure enough, the hunter came back again a few days later and, in his usual way, he imitated the sound of a bird to gather them together, then threw his net over them. Then said one bird, "You think you're so clever. Now's your time; lift away." The other retorted, "They say last time you lifted the net, both your wings moulted. Let's see you do it properly this time!"

But of course, while they were each telling the other one to lift the net, the hunter himself lifted it for them and crammed them in a heap into his basket and carried them off home, so that his wife's face was wreathed with smiles.

"So you see, my friends," said the Buddha, "quarrels amongst family and friends are a terrible thing, and lead only to destruction."

While Peace Reigns

Genre
traditional story; story from another culture

RE objectives

◆ To develop familiarity with a Buddhist way of telling legends.
◆ To discuss co-operation and working together.

Previous knowledge

Basic knowledge of who the Buddha was would be useful.

Background notes

This is an explicitly didactic story (see the Introduction, page 7), told to make a moral point, but given a context in the life of the Buddha, Siddhartha Gautama. It is one of many such stories known as the Jataka Tales. In each one the Buddha comments on a situation, often his disciples' behaviour, by telling a story. The story within the story has all the hallmarks of a fable whose truth claim is in its message, not its historicity. Yet within a Buddhist understanding of the world, there is an invitation in the final paragraph to believe that the story within a story did actually take place. However, many would draw a clear distinction between this sort of story and history. The historical element is the conviction that this is a story told by the Buddha.

This is a story which could stand on its own as a fable, but clearly children will need a reminder or an explanation of who the Buddha is, if it is not studied in connection with a unit of work on Buddhism.

Key words

Buddha; quarrels.

Discussing the text

◆ Read through the first two paragraphs to set the scene and the context.
◆ Read the story, asking the children to imagine each scene as you go along.
◆ Check the plot of the story by asking the children to recount it.
◆ Ask the children about the link between the opening scene and the story of the birds.
◆ What do the children think the Buddha was trying to teach his disciples? Was he trying to warn them of anything?
◆ Is there a message in the story for people today?
◆ What does the story tell us about the Buddha and Buddhist beliefs?
◆ Note that there are three quarrels in the story. What are they about? Who are they between? (The Buddha's disciples, the hunter and his wife, and the birds.)
◆ Divide the story into scenes. Ask the children to draw each one in a cartoon strip and give a title to each.

Further RE activities

◆ Read other stories about the Buddha and his teachings (in this book and see the Resources list, page 160).

◆ Discuss why people (and animals) quarrel. What are the consequences of quarrelling? (Warning! Be careful you teach and don't preach – let the children discuss the question.) Ask the children to suggest strategies for resolving disagreements and draw up a procedure for resolving quarrels.

◆ If it arises, discuss the ambiguity in historical status of some religious stories (see the Background notes above and the Introduction, page 7).

Further literacy ideas

◆ Look at the idea that there are two linked stories here. How are they linked? What actions and characters are similar in each story? Introduce the term 'parable' for this type of story with a meaning. Look at the way that fables and parables often have an implied 'warning' in their conclusion. Look at other fables (see below).

◆ Identify features which indicate that the story is from another culture – for example, the reference to the Buddha, bird-catching for a living, and so on.

◆ Look at the phrase 'many lifetimes ago'. What does it suggest? What other words can be used to suggest the distant past, or that the story took place in a different sort of time as in myth, legend or fable? Children might make up their own expressions.

◆ Pick out where the author has used repetition to remind the reader or listener of something that happened earlier.

◆ Ask the children to pick out all the words in the story indicating disagreement and tension, and to suggest other ones.

◆ Encourage them to pick out all the verbs in the story, then sort them into categories, such as those to do with speech, those to do with action, those to do with thinking or feeling, or other different categories chosen by the children.

◆ Look at the use of the past, present and future forms of verbs.

◆ Look at the animals speaking in the story. What other stories do they know in which animals speak, including fiction, such as the novels of CS Lewis and Dick King-Smith?

◆ Read other examples where a story about animals is used to teach about human behaviour, for example, Aesop's Fables or 'The Dog and the Cat' creation story in this book (see page 112).

◆ Discuss the point of view of the story. Then ask the children to rewrite it from the point of view of the hunter or his wife.

◆ Arrange the children in small groups to write a scene in which two people are quarrelling (perhaps in the form of a playscript). The scripts are then swapped and the children write two conclusions – one in which the quarrel remains unresolved; the other illustrating ways of making peace.

Memories of a Buddhist Childhood

Genre non-fiction: autobiography

About the author

Tshering Lama was born in Nepal. After she finished her studies in India, she worked as an air hostess for four years. She is now working for the World Wide Fund for Nature in Nepal.

As a child, I was very devout worshipper of our deities. We had a separate room kept as the chapel in our house, and it had a beautiful shrine. The statue of Guru Rimpoche occupied the central place of the shrine. He was our most respected Buddhist teacher who transformed Tibet into a Buddhist nation. The other statue was that of the Buddha. Then there were statues of other deities, various religious objects and photographs of the Dalai Lama and other living Buddhist teachers. Every morning my grandmother used to place seven silver bowls and fill them with water from a carved silver water jug. Then she lit the special butter lamp. This was followed by burning incense. When my brother and I were very young we were taught to prostrate before our shrine. Every morning and every evening before going to bed, we would prostrate three times on the ground before the shrine. As I prostrated, I would pray deeply, promising to be good and asking for a number of wishes to be fulfilled. All the teachers, the deities and Lord Buddha himself, were Gods to me at that early age and I loved them dearly.

My parents and other family elders would tell us Buddhist stories and other stories of human kindness. I cannot recall who told us Lord Buddha's story, but I knew it as a child. I remember my mother read us many religious stories. Many of these were Hindu stories for we lived in a very Hindu part of Nepal and to her all religions were the same. Sometimes she read to us directly from the Hindu holy books of the Bhagavad Gita and Mahabharata. So we learned to respect other religions. Our religion teaches us to be kind, and I learned this mainly through the example of acts of kindness around me. Somewhere along the way, I knew that as a Buddhist it was very important to be kind to others.

However, the Tibetan Buddhist community to which my family belongs does not have religious teachings made easy for children to understand. We learned what we could informally from our elders as we grew up. The Buddhist monks would chant their prayers and go away. There was never time to explain children's doubts and questions. Perhaps this was why, for a time as a teenager with a very questioning mind, I did not believe in religion. This was, no doubt, also partly due to the fact that the deities and even Buddha himself did not grant the wishes I had fervently prayed for. Then for many years I was unsure of what to believe in.

But for the last seven years I have been a practising Buddhist. I believe in the Buddhist teachings and I need them to help me live a better life. The teachings have helped me through pain and confusion. They have helped me to take pleasure in the good that life has to offer. They teach me to feel for and help those whom I can, and to think beyond my own needs. I pray to the deities sometimes but I no longer ask for wishes to be fulfilled. My praying today is to show homage and love for they belong to my family's history and traditions. I sometimes pray to them and to the Buddha for strength.

Tshering Tenpa Lama, 13 January 2000

Memories of a Buddhist Childhood

Genre
non-fiction: autobiography

RE objective

◆ To highlight the practice of the Buddhist faith.

Previous knowledge

None is strictly necessary as the text could be used as a starting point for studying Buddhism.

Background notes

Here is a very personal account of growing up in a Buddhist home, which describes some widely held practices. More significantly, it reflects the author's attitude to her faith.

Key words

Prostrate; deity; Hindu; Buddhist; Nepal.

Discussing the text

◆ Discuss the title and the idea of autobiography. What can we tell about the author just from the title, her name, and the little biographical note?

◆ Read the opening paragraph. What does it tell us about? (The shrine, what happened each day, the author's attitude.) Alternatively, ask the children to tell you something that they learned about the author as a child. Check the children understand the meaning of deities (god, gods or any being that is worshipped) and prostrate (to kneel or lie with one's face to the ground).

◆ Read the second paragraph. What is it about? What do we learn about the author's family? What was her mother's attitude to other religions? What do we learn about Buddhist teaching?

◆ Read the third paragraph. What was the author's attitude as a teenager? How was it different from when she was younger? Why did it change?

◆ Read the final paragraph. What does the author feel about Buddhism now? How is it different from when she was a child and then a teenager? How does Buddhism help her?

◆ Encourage the children to respond to the text and have an open discussion about it.

Further RE activities

◆ Read the story of the Buddha and find out about his teachings (see 'The Four Noble Truths', page 12).

◆ Bring in a statue or statues of the Buddha. Ask the children to make an observational drawing of it and/or to look at pictures of Buddhist shrines.

◆ Draw the children's attention to any news items about the Dalai Lama.

◆ How have the children's beliefs changed since they were younger? (This need not be about religion. Examples might be: Father Christmas or the tooth fairy, or 'Once I thought my aunt lived at Sainsbury's. Now I know she lives in Salisbury.') Allow the children to respond first, and only make suggestions if they have difficulty.

◆ Discuss different reasons why people pray, and different ways of praying.

◆ Give the children the opportunity to discuss what they find hard to understand about religious teachings, or used to find hard about religion.

◆ Discuss places in the home for quiet reflection, religious artefacts in their homes. Make a quiet corner for reflection in the classroom.

Further literacy ideas

◆ Suggest the children draw three pictures: one of how they imagine the author as a child; one as a teenager; one as an adult. They can then add a thought bubble containing something to show how she is thinking about her religion at the time.

◆ Identify all the words and phrases that indicate time, for example, 'as a child', 'every morning'. Look at the use of the past and present tenses.

◆ Ask the children to suggest a heading for each paragraph, for example, 'How I worshipped as a child' for the first paragraph.

◆ Encourage the children to describe something which either they did when they were younger, or which happens in the home or school now, for example, observation of a festival or school assemblies. It should be something that happens, or happened, repeatedly so they can write about the general practice and not the particular situation.

The Life of a Zen Buddhist Nun

About the author

Genre
autobiographical

Martine Batchelor was born in France. She spent ten years as a Zen Buddhist nun in South Korea, and since her return to the UK in 1985, has lived in Devonshire where she works as a lecturer, spiritual counsellor, meditation teacher and writer.

I became a Zen Buddhist nun in Korea because I wanted to meditate. I felt the need to transform my mind and my emotions. When I read a Buddhist book, I realized that meditation could help me to do that.

In Korea, there are temples for studying Buddhist books (sutras), others for chanting and serving the lay people and others that put more emphasis on meditation practice. Songkwangsa Temple is one of the major monasteries in the whole country, offering many Buddhist activities but it was most well known for meditation. A great Zen master, Master Kusan, was living there and he encouraged me to become a nun.

Before becoming a nun, first I had to be a postulant for six months, working in the fields and in the kitchen, learning the chants and the ceremonies, the Buddhist way of life of a monastery and how to meditate.

Throughout the day we followed the signals of various bells. Getting up at three o'clock in the morning was sometimes a little difficult. At that time we went to the temple to chant, to greet the day. I loved the special morning chant which was about well-wishing. It said:

May the ocean of goodness from our practice return to the world to fulfil its purpose.

May the world rest in peace and the wheel of the Buddhist Law revolve.

May each being that is born rest in wisdom and never fall back.

May this wisdom be as fierce and courageous as a Buddha's.

May we attain the fruit of great awakening...

The meditation started soon after. First we sat for fifty minutes and then we walked for ten minutes. We did this ten or twelve times throughout the day. The point of the meditation was to focus the mind on a question and ask this question: 'What is this?" as deeply as we could. We were not supposed to analyze or look for an answer but just to ask unconditionally. Concentration on the question helped me to become more calm and still. Asking the question helped my mind to become clearer and sharper.

One of the effects of the meditation that I noticed very quickly was that I started to become more aware of myself and others and also became more caring. Suddenly, I could not kill mosquitoes or flies anymore because I realized that they had as much the wish and the right to live as I had. So I contrived a device. Every evening I caught them with a glass and a postcard and I took them out of the meditation room.

Every fifteen days, as we followed the lunar calendar, we used to have a hot bath and shave our head. The following day we recited the monks and nuns' precepts. The monks and nuns' precepts encouraged us to live a pure and clean life, very simple and non-harming to ourselves or others. They require the monks and the nuns to be celibate (not to marry) and to abstain from killing, stealing, lying and taking alcohol.

Alternatively we recited the Bodhisattva's precepts. A Bodhisattva in Zen Buddhism is someone who makes the vow to help everyone, and not to cause suffering to oneself or to others. These precepts emphasized the caring and the giving of life. They inspired us to be generous, disciplined and compassionate. They also helped us to reflect, to look into the causes and effects of our actions. Why do we do what we do? Is it for our own selfish reasons? Is it for the well-being of others? Can it be for both? These precepts remind us that compassion is essential to the Buddhist path.

After the precept ceremony each lunar month, the Zen master used to give a talk. He encouraged us to practise hard, to continue to develop wisdom and compassion. Most importantly he urged us to awaken to our true nature which was exactly the same as the Buddha. Afterwards we would go to the master's

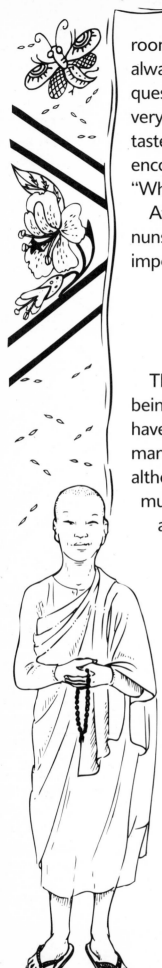

room and I translated the talk for the other Westerners. He always gave us some nice tea and cakes. Sometimes he asked us questions like, "Do you like the tea?" "Yes we love the tea, it is very good," we would reply. Then he would say: "What is it that tastes the tea?" We could never answer to his satisfaction and he encouraged us to concentrate more intensely on the question: "What is this?"

At the end of the master's talk, the whole assembly of monks, nuns and lay people used to recite the Four Vows which are very important for Zen Buddhists:

> *Living beings are numberless, I vow to save them all.*
> *Confusions are countless, I vow to eliminate them all.*
> *The Buddha's teachings are limitless, I vow to master them all.*
> *The Buddha's way is endless, I vow to achieve it.*

These vows are to inspire us to practise for the sake of all beings. They remind us that there is a lot of work to do as we have many confusions to clear up. They point out that there are many different methods to help us on the way. And finally, although the Buddha's way is great and sometimes difficult, we must be determined and have the confidence that we can achieve it. We can develop more and more wisdom and compassion so that we can be of benefit to ourselves and the whole world.

Glossary

lay people people who follow a religion but have not taken vows as monks, nuns, priests or ministers.

meditation a form of reflective, concentrated thinking

precepts commands, moral teachings

postulant someone who lives in a monastery or nunnery because he/she wants to become a monk or nun. Postulants begin to practise the life of a monk or nun but have not taken the vows.

Zen Buddhism a form of Buddhism widely practised in China, Japan and Korea.

The Life of a Zen Buddhist Nun

Genre
autobiographical

RE objectives

◆ To learn about the life of a Buddhist monk or nun.

◆ To consider the benefits of reflection.

Previous knowledge

Some knowledge of Buddhism would be useful.

Background notes

This text conveys some information about the daily life of a nun or monk and, more importantly, demonstrates that this daily life is rooted in the conviction that meditation and questioning helps to transform the person in order to serve others. The paragraph describing the meditation will probably puzzle more than explain. It is something learned by participation not by description.

The text can easily be divided into two sections if you consider there is too much in it for one day. The first half is very general. The second, beginning 'Every fifteen days' focuses on the precept ceremony.

Key words

Monk; nun; Buddhist temple; chant; meditation; Bodhisattva; Zen master.

Discussing the text

◆ Unfamiliar words can be tackled by using the glossary, by looking at the context and, if necessary, with the use of a dictionary.

◆ Read the first section: look at the title. Ask the children to pool and discuss prior knowledge about Buddhism, monks and nuns. (Some children may well have met Roman Catholic nuns.) You might note that this is a description of a monastery in South Korea, and find South Korea on a map.

◆ Look at the first paragraph, noting that the account is autobiographical and written in the first person. What reason does the author give for wanting to become a nun? What do the children think the word 'transform' means here?

◆ Why did she choose Songkwangsa Temple?

◆ Encourage the children to form a mental picture of what she did throughout the day. What else did she do besides meditation and chanting?

◆ Concentrate on the time the day started and how it was begun, rather than the content of the chant.

◆ Similarly, in the next paragraph, concentrate on the amount of meditation, the sitting and walking rather than the questions asked.

◆ Read the next section. The author tells us she changed through meditation. In what way did she change?

◆ Now re-read the first section, focusing on different parts of the text, for instance the morning chant: why do the children think it is called a well-wishing chant?

◆ Ask the children to suggest interpretations for each line. What images are conjured up? Why an 'ocean of goodness'? Some may recall the story of the Buddha in the line about awakening.

◆ Re-read the section about meditation, and gain the children's response – which is likely to be that they can't grasp it. Discuss the difficulty of describing action. We can talk about riding a bike or swimming, but you can't really understand it until you can do it yourself.

◆ Read the second section: point out that this is telling us about something that happened every fifteen days. Unravel the link to the lunar month (that is, that the ceremony took place at the new moon and the full moon). Read the rest of the paragraph. How did the monks and nuns prepare for the ceremony?

◆ During the initial reading, tell the children that you will concentrate on what happened at the ceremonies. Read through the passage in one go and then pick out the sections that describe what took place.

◆ Re-read the second section: look back through the rest of the text, focusing more closely on what the author is saying about:

– the life of a nun

– whose teaching the nun follows

– Buddhist teachings – these are expressed in a very abstract way. Nevertheless, children can pick out and discuss key words such as 'wisdom' and 'compassion'.

Further RE activities

◆ Find out more about the life of the Sangha, the Buddhist community. Organize a visit to a local Buddhist community if there is one nearby.

◆ Re-read the story of the Buddha and his first disciples, for example in *A Tapestry of Tales* (see the Resources list, page 160) and ask the children to think in what ways the nun's life follows the Buddha's example.

◆ Re-read the story of the Four Noble Truths and the Eightfold Path (page 12), and ask the children to think about how the nun is following the Eightfold Path.

◆ Encourage the children to write as though they were a visitor to a monastery or temple. What would they expect to see?

◆ Write well-wishing chants to start the day.

◆ Discuss the value of sitting still and thinking and reflecting. How is this different from sitting still in front of the television or staring out of the window in class?

◆ Discuss the things that we do inside our heads, such as dreaming, imagining, hoping and so on. Do our thoughts make a difference to the way we behave?

◆ Discuss vows and promises. What vows do people make when they join other organizations, for example the Guides, the Scouts or the army, or make to other people, such as during marriage? Can we make vows to ourselves?

Further literacy ideas

◆ Look at the composition of words such as 'unconditionally'. Which word is at the centre? How does the meaning and function of the word change with the addition of each prefix and suffix? Experiment with the addition of 'un-' to other words, (some of which will 'work' others will not), such as 'happy', 'sad', 'faithful', 'grateful', 'welcome', 'wet', 'clever' and 'intelligent'.

◆ Also try the activity with other prefixes and suffixes, such as 'dis-', 'mis-', 're-', '-less' and '-ful'.

◆ Look at the phrases that show that an activity was regular and repeated, for example 'every fifteen days' or 'each lunar month'. How would the meaning change if it was written, 'after the first fifteen days' or 'at the end of that month'?

◆ How are quotations indicated in the layout?

◆ This is an autobiographical text. How is it different from a text written in the third person? Alter the text so that it is written in the third person. Look at the sections which show the feelings and attitudes of a particular person.

◆ Ask the children to write a first person text about routines in an earlier part of their life (for example when they were in an earlier class).

Christianity

The first Christians were Jews who were followers of a man called Jesus whom they believed to be the Messiah promised in the Jewish scriptures. Thus the early church adopted the Jewish scriptures as their own, although with some controversy. These scriptures came to be known as the Old Testament because it was believed they spoke of the covenant with God which pertained to the time before the coming of Jesus. They included the first five books of Moses (the Torah – see 'Judaism', page 93) the Psalms and other books in a variety of genre. The Psalms in the Bible have a significant place in the worship of most Christian churches, in addition to other readings from the Bible.

The early church soon produced its own documents. First there were letters from Church leaders, particularly Paul, who took the Christian message beyond the borders of Palestine to the Gentiles (non-Jews) in the Graeco-Roman world. The letter to the Christians in Corinth (see page 41) was probably written about AD57. The Gospels began to appear around AD70. These were narratives of the life and teachings of Jesus, based on a strong oral tradition and some earlier writings.

For some Christians, such as Protestant fundamentalists, it is important that the Bible is literally true in all aspects. For others, including the Roman Catholic Church, it is true in all matters of doctrine. For yet others, the Bible is a powerful witness to communities working out their faith, reflecting the beliefs of the time but also speaking powerfully to human experience today. However, these issues are not central to this volume since we have opted for a poetic text in selecting an example from the sacred writings of the religion.

The Bible was written in at least two languages, Hebrew and Greek, but, unlike the traditions of Islam and Judaism, no great emphasis was ever placed on reading it in the original language. It was the message about Jesus that was deemed to be important, not the particular words themselves. The debate about literary merit in translating the Bible is one which continues to this day, and is especially relevant when looking at a poem from the Bible.

The Bible has given rise to many other stories and legends, including numerous retellings for children. We have included here, as an example, a legend arising from the story of the wise men visiting the infant Jesus. While the Bible is the touchstone of the Christian faith – its sacred book – there are many other texts which reflect and shape Christian tradition. It may be that the theology of most Christians is formed more from the hymns which are a regular part of their worship than from the Bible itself. Traditional prayers, such as those from the Celtic tradition included here, have also been a part of Christian literature, and stories of the lives of Christians down the ages, whether legendary or historical, form an important part of Christian tradition.

A Hymn to Love

Genre
poetry

If I speak in the tongues of men and of angels, but have not love, I am a noisy gong or a clanging cymbal.

And if I have prophetic powers, and understand all mysteries and all knowledge, and if I have all faith, so as to remove mountains, but have not love, I am nothing.

If I give away all I have, and if I deliver my body to be burned, but have not love, I gain nothing.

Love is patient and kind; love is not jealous or boastful; it is not arrogant or rude. Love does not insist on its own way; it is not irritable or resentful;
it does not rejoice at wrong, but rejoices in the right. Love bears all things, believes all things, hopes all things, endures all things.

Love never ends; as for prophecies, they will pass away; as for tongues, they will cease; as for knowledge, it will pass away.

For our knowledge is imperfect and our prophecy is imperfect;
but when the perfect comes, the imperfect will pass away. When I was a child, I spoke like a child, I thought like a child, I reasoned like a child; when I became a man, I gave up childish ways.
For now we see in a mirror dimly, but then face to face. Now I know in part; then I shall understand fully, even as I have been fully understood.

So faith, hope, love abide, these three; but the greatest of these is love.

I Corinthians 13 (Revised Standard Version)

A Hymn to Love

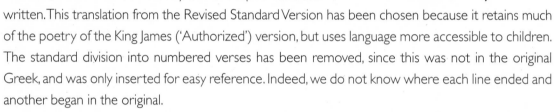

Genre
poetry

RE objective

◆ To develop an understanding of the
Christian concept of love.

Previous knowledge

None needed.

Background notes

This hymn to love, from Paul's first letter to
the Corinthians, comes from one of the earliest
books of the New Testament. It was written originally
in Greek, around AD57, before any of the Gospels had been
written. This translation from the Revised Standard Version has been chosen because it retains much
of the poetry of the King James ('Authorized') version, but uses language more accessible to children.
The standard division into numbered verses has been removed, since this was not in the original
Greek, and was only inserted for easy reference. Indeed, we do not know where each line ended and
another began in the original.

Although the rhythm of the original language cannot be recreated in translation, the rhythm and
flow of ideas, the setting of one idea against its opposite, the balance of the sentences, is very
reminiscent of the Hebrew poetry of the psalms.

Key words

Love.

Discussing the text

◆ Introduce the poem by reminding the children that in the story of 'Sleeping Beauty', the princess's
fairy godmothers made wishes that she would grow up with all sorts of gifts and talents. Can the
children suggest what these might be?

◆ Now tell the class that in the poem you are about to read, the poet says that the most important
gift a person can have or give to another is that of love. Read the poem to them, perhaps twice, so
that the balancing phrases in the poem can sink in. Then give them a copy of the text so that they can
refer to it.

◆ Ask the children how the poet suggests to the reader that love is the most important thing of all.
Encourage them to look at the beginning and the end of the poem. What other things does he seem
to think are valuable but useless without love? Ask them what they think it means to speak with the
tongues of angels (that is, eloquently).

◆ Wonder with the children why the poet talks about being a child.

◆ Suggest to them that the poet then pictures love as a person. Pick out the key words and phrases
which describe how love would behave if love were a person. Explore with the children why being
patient and kind might be characteristics of love. Do they agree with the writer that these are the
characteristics of love? Ask the children what sort of behaviour he is encouraging in his readers.

◆ Tell the children that this poem is often read at weddings, but raise the question whether the poet is talking about two people who have 'fallen in love' or something other or bigger than that (the poet himself was unmarried).

◆ Read the poem again.

Further RE activities

◆ Put the poem in the context of the Bible, explaining it is part of a letter written by one of the earliest Christians. Christians believe that Jesus exemplified love. Ask the children to recall stories they know about Jesus, which show him as loving.

◆ Look at the story of the Good Samaritan (Luke 10: 23–37) as an illustration of what it is to love your neighbour. Discuss whether the poem and the parable of the Good Samaritan suggest that loving is about the way you feel or about the way you behave. What do the children think? Can you love someone you don't know?

◆ Study examples of Christians who have sought to live out these words fully in their lives: Mother Theresa is one obvious example, and you could also look at saints both ancient and modern (St Francis extended his love to animals as well as people).

◆ Discuss some loving ways to behave in today's world.

◆ The poem says that love is patient and kind. Discuss with the children whether they think there are situations when we shouldn't be patient and kind. Should a victim be patient with a bully, for example?

Further literacy ideas

◆ Look at all the different ways the word 'love' is used in English, with both weak and strong meanings. Ask the children to consider differences in what people mean when a person says 'I love baked beans' or 'I love football', when a boy says 'I love you' to a girl and a mother says 'I love you' to a child. Look at other words for love, such as 'adore'.

◆ Tell the children that the poem is a translation. Compare one or two verses from this translation with other translations, such as the Good News Bible, Jerusalem Bible and King James (Authorized Version) and look at the different choices of words. Note that in the King James version (so-called because it was written in the time of King James I), the word 'charity' was used instead of 'love'. Discuss what 'charity' means now.

◆ Ask the children to write their own versions of the first three verses, substituting skills which they believe are of value.

◆ Suggest the children write their own personifications modelled on the poem, for example,

Anger is…

Hope is…

Friendship is…

◆ Encourage the children to write their own poems about love.

◆ Ask them to write a story in which someone acts with loving kindness.

◆ Begin a class collection of poems with the theme of love, discussing differences between them in the perception of love.

How Great Thou Art

O Lord my God
When I in awesome wonder
Consider all the works Thy hands have made.
I see the stars, I hear the rolling thunder,
Thy power throughout the universe displayed
Then sings my soul,
My Saviour God, to Thee:
How great thou art
How great art.

When through the woods and forest glades I wander
And hear the birds sing sweetly in the trees;
When I look down from lofty mountain grandeur,
And hear the brook, and feel the gently breeze,
Then sings my soul,
My Saviour God, to Thee:
How great thou art
How great art.

by Stuart K Hine

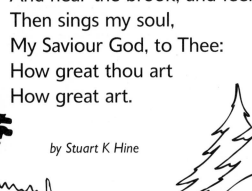

How Great Thou Art

Re objectives

◆ To develop the idea that praise is important in Christian worship.

◆ To look at the concept of God creating the world.

Previous knowledge

None needed.

Background notes

This text can be studied alongside the hymns of praise from Judaism (page 99) and Sikhism (page 147); all three hymns link God with creation, albeit with different focuses. Each one could be studied on a separate day in sequence. Here, a person stands in awe of nature; it is an expression of his wonder, praising God as creator himself, rather than calling on others to praise as well. This is part of a Russian Orthodox hymn from the 19th century, made popular by an English translation in the 20th century.

It is usually sung with an organ, piano or sometimes guitar accompaniment, although in its original Russian form it would have been unaccompanied.

Discussing the text

◆ Introduce the text simply as a poem, then read through it as a whole.

◆ Ask the children for their first responses. What do they think the poet was feeling about life and about nature when he wrote these verses? What sort of mood was he in? What is it that suggests it might be a song? Where do they think it might be sung and when might it be sung?

◆ Return to the poem/hymn to look at individual phrases and words. Discuss the meaning of 'awesome' and 'wonder'. Is the author wondering in the sense of being curious, or is it something else? Does the author picture God as a big man with big hands – and if not, why does he say 'the works Thy hands have made'? What do the children understand by the term 'soul' in the text? (Note that there can be no definition of this.)

◆ How might God's power link to the rolling thunder? (See also the Jewish blessing on hearing thunder on page 102.)

◆ Allow some time for the children to discuss their own views and feelings on thunder. Do they think that the writer is necessarily saying that at that point in time God is making that bit of thunder?

◆ Ask them whether people of other religions than Christianity could sing this song. Why?

◆ Encourage them to discuss their own feelings about the natural world. What sort of things make them want to say: 'That's wonderful or beautiful'. Is there anything which frightens or disturbs them? (For example they might say spiders.)

Further RE activities

◆ Learn more about Christian worship, both in church and in other contexts, for example by videoing part of *Songs of Praise* and discussing it with the children.

◆ Using one or more hymn books, find further hymns of praise from a subject index, or find hymns with other themes.

◆ Have a circle time in which children finish the sentence, 'I felt awe/wonder when I…'

◆ Discuss whether all people who feel awe in the presence of something beautiful or intriguing always believe in God (this would need to be a very open discussion).

◆ Compare this with the other hymns of praise (see 'Psalm 148' on page 99 and 'A Hymn of Praise from Guru Nanak' on page 147). Here are three authors from three different times and religions. What beliefs and attitudes do they appear to have in common? (Belief in God is a starting point.)

Further literacy ideas

◆ Explore further the meanings of the words 'wonder' and 'awe'. What happens to them when the suffix '-ful' is added? The word 'awe' seems to completely change its meaning. (King James II is reputed to have said that St Paul's Cathedral was an awful building – meaning it provoked awe.)

◆ Look at the archaic form 'Thou art'. Compare it with the first person and third person forms of pronouns and verb 'to be'.

◆ Look at the use of capital letters.

Susan's Diary

by Susan Fisher

Genre
non-fiction: personal writing/diary

Monday, 28 Sept

My sister got baptized last night. I had to go. Mum made me. I didn't want to. Ann kept fussing about what to wear. Mum kept saying, "I don't see why — surely it is what's inside that's important and if you're such a good Christian, I think you could help me more with the washing up." I think she could too.

Dad kept saying she didn't need to get baptized because she had been baptized as a baby but she said that didn't count because she didn't know or understand anything when she was a baby, and now she wanted to show everybody that she believed in Jesus.

In the end she wore that new mini-skirt she got last week. Don't know why she bothered. They dressed her up in a long white robe when it came to the baptism. She looked very solemn.

I was surprised at the chapel hall. It was quite different to when we have Sunday school. They moved the table with flowers on it over to the side, and lifted the platform lid up. Underneath there was a pool with water. I don't think the water is there all the time. They just fill it up like a big bath when there's a baptism.

There was lots of singing and prayers first. There was a long sermon by a man with ginger hair who shouted quite a bit. Then it was time for the baptism. There were three of them — Ann, John and Eva. Ann went first. She stepped down into the water. They must have heated the water because she didn't hesitate when she went in.

Mr Jackson said to her, "Ann, have you accepted the Lord Jesus Christ as your own personal saviour?"

She said, "I have."

And then he said, "I baptize you in the name of the Father, Son and Holy Spirit."

He put one hand round her waist and one hand on her forehead and she leaned backwards into the water with an almighty splash.

Afterwards she came out dripping, but with a big smile on her face and everyone sang a chorus, "Trust and obey, for there's no other way to be happy in Jesus but to trust and obey."

Afterwards we all went to the back hall for tea and cakes and biscuits, and then I had an argument with Mum because I said I wanted to go home on the Church bus with my Sunday school friends but she said it was late and I had to go in the car with her.

Susan's Diary

Genre
*non-fiction:
personal
writing/diary*

RE objectives
◆ To develop knowledge of the Christian rite of baptism.
◆ To look at how we show commitment.

Previous knowledge
None needed.

Background notes
Adult Christian baptism is practised among a number of Christian denominations, including the Baptists and the Open Brethren. This baptism took place in an Open Brethren gospel hall. In contrast, most Christian churches baptize babies and young children: promises are made on their behalf by parents and godparents and confirmed when they are older. Adult or Believer's baptism is seen as an affirmation of faith by the candidate, whereas infant baptism is a sacrament whereby the child becomes a member of the Christian church. There are no priests or vicars in the Open Brethren; baptisms are performed by lay members of the congregation. Learning about the different Baptismal rites helps children to recognize the diversity within Christianity.

Key words
Baptism.

Discussing the text
◆ Introduce the text simply as a diary entry and read it with the children. Ask them what the author is recording and encourage them to talk about their own knowledge and experiences of baptism. How were they similar to and different from the account here? Why does Ann say she wants to be baptised?
◆ Ask the children to suggest what age they think the two girls might be, and why. Do they think the parents also go to the same chapel? Encourage the children to suggest the feelings and attitudes of each character before they set out for the chapel.
◆ Consider with the children what the mother may have meant by saying 'it is what's inside that's important'.
◆ Look at the statement 'Father, Son and Holy Spirit'. What is this referring to? If necessary, explain that Christians talk about God as God the Father, God the Son (Jesus), and God the Holy Spirit.
◆ Discuss what can be learned about the practice of Baptism in this particular church from this passage.
◆ Ask them to write an account as if they were Ann.

Further RE activities
◆ Read to the class or ask them to look up themselves the story of Jesus's baptism in the Bible, Mark 1: 4–11.

◆ Look with the children at infant baptism and christening. If appropriate, ask them to bring in some christening photos. Ask them to find out about christenings from information books.

◆ Ask the children to work in small groups to discuss what makes a good Christian, and then report back in a plenary.

◆ Look at the ways in which people show their commitment to a group or belief, for example, Brownie promises, Sikh turban, football shirts.

Further literacy ideas

◆ Make a class glossary of words to do with worship and the church (a few are in the text, such as 'chapel', 'sermon' and 'baptism').

◆ Note that this is an edited version of the text. The original diary might not have had complete punctuation marks, and these have been added later. Nevertheless, look at the use of speech marks. Discuss with the children why people take less care about punctuation in a diary than they might do for work in school.

◆ Discuss why people keep diaries, noting that very conscientious diary keepers write about everything that affects them that day, and about ordinary days not just special ones.

◆ Look at some of the features common in diary writing, such as opinions being given, the use of the first person, and no explanations given to the reader even though the passage contains narrative and description. Point out, however, that diary writing varies according to the age of the writer and the degree of self-consciousness in the writing. Some diarists even write with an audience in mind.

◆ Find other examples of diary writing, such as the diary of Anne Frank or that of Samuel Pepys.

◆ Ask the children to write a diary entry about something that happened the previous day, or a memory of a baptism they have attended.

Prayers from the Celtic Tradition

Taken from Carmina Gadelica, edited by Alexander Carmichael (Floris Books, Edinburgh 1992)

Genre

poetry – including prayer and poetry from different places and times

A Prayer for Night Shielding

My God and my Chief,
I seek to Thee in the morning,
My God and my Chief,
I seek to Thee this night.
I am giving Thee my mind,
I am giving Thee my will,
My soul everlasting and my body.

Mayest Thou be chieftain over me,
Mayest Thou be master unto me,
Mayest Thou be shepherd over me,
Mayest Thou be guardian unto me,
Mayest Thou be herdsman over me,
Mayest Thou be guide unto me,
Mayest Thou be with me, O Chief of chiefs,
Father everlasting and God of the heavens.

Collector's Note

The reciter said that she heard this hymn, and many other hymns and songs, tunes and melodies, when a child, from her father John MacNeill and from her mother Mary Maclean. Her parents had innumerable songs and hymns, chants and melodies, which they taught to their children. She, however, was but a child when her parents died, and she remembers but fragments of what they taught to her and her brothers and sisters. The woman taught all that she could remember of her childhood's prayers and hymns and harmonies to her own ten children, most of whom are now dead. The woman said that she often thought over those old songs and airs, hymns and tunes, that she heard in her childhood and never heard again since, and that they appear to her very peculiar and very different from anything that she had ever heard since then. She thinks that most of them must have been very old; they were very weird and very beautiful.

A Prayer for Smooring the Fire

The sacred Three
To save,
To shield,
To surround
The hearth,
The house,
The household,
This eve,
This night,
Oh! this eve,
This night,
And every night,
Each single night.
Amen.

The Protection of Cattle

Pastures smooth, long, and spreading,
Grassy meads aneath your feet,
The friendship of God the Son to bring you home
To the field of the fountains,
Field of the fountains.

Closed be every pit to you,
Smoothed be every knoll to you,
Cosy every exposure to you,
Beside the cold mountains,
Beside the cold mountains.

The care of Peter and of Paul,
The care of James and of John,
The care of Bride fair and of Mary Virgin.
To meet you and to tend you.
Oh! the care of all the band
To protect you and to strengthen you.

Prayers from the Celtic Tradition

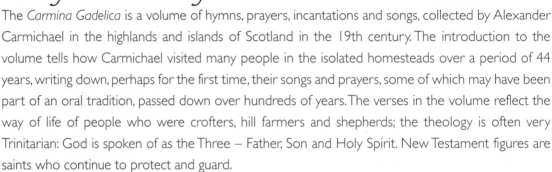

Genre

poetry – including prayer and poetry from different places and times

RE objectives

◆ To develop familiarity with the range of prayers.

◆ To learn some reasons why people pray.

Previous knowledge

Some knowledge of Christianity would be useful.

Background knowledge

The *Carmina Gadelica* is a volume of hymns, prayers, incantations and songs, collected by Alexander Carmichael in the highlands and islands of Scotland in the 19th century. The introduction to the volume tells how Carmichael visited many people in the isolated homesteads over a period of 44 years, writing down, perhaps for the first time, their songs and prayers, some of which may have been part of an oral tradition, passed down over hundreds of years. The verses in the volume reflect the way of life of people who were crofters, hill farmers and shepherds; the theology is often very Trinitarian: God is spoken of as the Three – Father, Son and Holy Spirit. New Testament figures are saints who continue to protect and guard.

Alexander Carmichael wrote, regarding 'A Prayer for Smooring the Fire': Peat is the fuel of the Highlands and Islands. Where wood is not obtainable, the fire is kept alive during the night by a special process. The process by which this is accomplished is called smaladh in Gaelic; smooring in Scottish and smothering (or more correctly, subduing) in English. The ceremony of smooring the fire is artistic and symbolic, and is performed with loving care. The embers are evenly spread on the hearth – which is generally in the middle of the floor – and formed into a circle. This circle is then divided into three equal sections, a small boss being left in the middle. A peat is laid between each section, each peat touching the boss, which forms a common centre. The first peat is laid down in name of the God of Life, the second in name of the God of Peace, the third in name of the God of Grace. The circle is then covered over with sufficient ashes to subdue but not to extinguish the fire, in name of the Three of Light.

These particular prayers show the earthiness of the Christian faith: God was connected with every aspect of life, from damping down the fire in the evening to prayers for the protection of cattle. These are not poems which were hidden away in a book on the shelf; these are poems and prayers which were known by heart, learned through hearing others say them, and regularly spoken in everyday situations as part of the fabric of life.

Copying one of the poems is suggested as an activity since there are times when copying can be a means of quiet meditation.

Key words

Prayer

Discussing the text

◆ The prayers can be studied separately or as a group.

◆ Introduce the texts by conjuring up the image of Alexander Carmichael who travelled the hills of Scotland visiting farmers and shepherds in their tiny cottages perched on hillsides and snuggled into villages. He asked them to recall the prayers they had been taught by their parents who had learned them, in turn, from their parents before them; he then wrote them down. Ask the children to suggest the sort of things people who were shepherds and hill farmers might have prayed for.

A Prayer for Night Shielding

◆ Look at the title and the choice of the word 'shield'. What images does it conjure up for the children? Do they think it is simply a question of protection? Read the prayer together, perhaps twice. Encourage an open response to the prayer, including encouraging the children to say how it made them feel.

◆ Look together at the detail of the prayer. Who is speaking? Who is being addressed? Apart from the title, how can we tell that it is a prayer for speaking at night?

◆ What does the speaker offer to God?

◆ What do they think the speaker is asking of God in each of the first six lines of the second verse? How might these roles relate to the idea that is a prayer for 'shielding'? In other words, how does a chieftain shield one? How does a shepherd shield one?

◆ Ask the children to consider how these ideas fit with their own ideas of God. (They do not have to believe in God, only to have ideas about God.)

◆ Why do they think that this was/is a prayer said in the evening?

◆ Read the children the collector's note to this prayer. Do they share the attitude that the prayer is different from other things they have heard?

A Prayer for Smooring the Fire

◆ Look at the title and the unusual word 'smooring'. Use the information given in 'Background knowledge' to discuss the importance of doing this at night.

◆ Look at who is being addressed. Who do the children think are 'The sacred Three'?

◆ Read though the prayer together and allow the children to make an initial response to what the speaker is asking. Note that it says nothing about damping down the fire. Why then the title? Why would these words be spoken at this time? Note also the image of the shield again. For what is the speaker asking protection and shielding? Discuss with them whether the prayer would have any meaning said today, even without a fire to 'smoor'.

The Protection of Cattle

◆ Look at title and read through poem. Who is being addressed? (That is, who is 'you'?)

◆ The speaker is wishing good things for his or her cattle. What is he or she wishing for them? What are the dangers that might befall them?

◆ Who are the people mentioned in the final verse? Encourage the children to talk about the protection of the saints.

(Note: Peter, James and John were three of Jesus's closest disciples and, with Paul who was converted after Jesus's death, they were the leaders of the early church. 'Bride fair' probably refers to Bride, also known as Bridget, a very popular saint in Celtic communities, sometimes regarded as the patron saint of domestic cattle.)

◆ Discuss with the children what they would want to keep safe. Who or what is important to them?

◆ Ask them to copy one of the prayers in their best handwriting and to make an appropriate decorative border. They could also be encouraged to learn one of them by heart, in keeping with the idea of an oral tradition.

Further RE activities

◆ If appropriate to the school context (for example, a Church of England School), ask the children to write their own prayers based on these prayers.

◆ Explore prayer further with the children by looking at other prayers, including prayers from other faiths (for example, Jewish blessings) and graces children may know from home or school, by considering when and where people pray, and by gathering pictures and artefacts connected with prayer. Discuss why people pray.

◆ Do further work with the children on Celtic Christianity, and about Bride and the other saints mentioned in 'The Protection of Cattle'.

◆ Look at the ways we wish people well today, such as, 'Have a nice day'. What do we wish and hope for others? What do we wish and hope for school, class, pets and so on, which we might want to express particularly at times of parting?

Further literacy ideas

◆ Look in detail as some of the linguistic features of the prayers:

– the archaic language in the poems, including the use of the second person singular form 'Thee'. Ask the children to suggest other old words that they know which suggest that something was written a long time ago.

– the metaphors, taken from the daily lives of the people. Discuss which people are the 'shielders' in the children's present-day world.

– the repetition in the verses and its function (for example, giving the verses unity and rhythm, as well as emphasising points).

– the line breaks, considering how different it is if one attempts to read it as continuous prose and whether it breaks the lines differently.

– in the first and last poem, look at how the division of verses corresponds to a shift in subject matter.

◆ Make a class collection of sayings and verses learned 'at the mother's knee' or in the playground, rather than those from a book, for example, nursery rhymes, and family sayings.

The Pilgrim's Hymn

Genre
poetry; hymn

Who would true valour see
Let him come hither;
One here will constant be,
Come wind, come weather;
There's no discouragement
Shall make him once relent
His first avowed intent
To be a pilgrim.

Who so beset him round
With dismal stories,
Do but themselves confound;
His strength the more is.
No lion can him fright,
He'll with a giant fight,
But he will have a right
To be a pilgrim.

Hobgoblin nor foul fiend
Can daunt his spirit;
He knows he at the end
Shall life inherit.
Then fancies fly away;
He'll fear not what men say;
He'll labour night and day
To be a pilgrim.

Glossary

valour personal courage (now chiefly used in poetry)

confound confuse or make someone look foolish

avowed declared

The Pilgrim's Hymn

Genre
poetry; hymn

RE objectives

◆ To develop familiarity with a major Christian hymn.

◆ To allow an opportunity to think about life as a pilgrimage.

◆ To reflect on doing your best.

Previous knowledge

None needed.

Background notes

The children may well have come across this hymn in a more modern, revised version. We have presented the original because of the power of its strong imagery. It is a poem based on the allegory of the Pilgrim's Progress; it symbolizes the idea that this life is a journey to the next. However, it need not be limited to this one meaning. Christianity has always had within it a double sense – that there is the kingdom of God to come in the future, but that the kingdom is also in the here and now. The pilgrimage is about living a better, fuller life on earth as well as journeying to another life.

Key words

Pilgrim; constant; strength.

Discussing the text

◆ First reading: start by looking at the title and discussing briefly what a pilgrim is, drawing on children's studies of pilgrimages to Mecca, and so on. You might draw out that a pilgrim can travel by himself or herself, or be part of a large group as in the case of the pilgrims to Mecca.

◆ Read through it as a whole once, and ask children for their first reactions. Then take each verse at a time.

◆ Read through the first verse. Do the children think that the poem was written recently or many years ago. Why?

◆ Help the children paraphrase this verse using the glossary. Tell them that the construction 'who would' means 'anyone who wants'.

◆ We are looking at 'one here' (the pilgrim) who is really brave, who has to be constant, loyal to his pilgrimage, who is encouraged to stick to his pilgrimage whatever the weather. What does that suggest about the journey?

◆ Ask the children to imagine someone setting out on a pilgrimage, a journey, through difficult weather. The way is likely to be hard going and difficult. What might his friends say to him or her?

◆ Read the second and third verses, in as dramatic a way as possible.

Whom does the pilgrim meet on his journey? Does he give into them? Are these the sort of beings normally met on a journey? What sorts of stories might the goblins and giants tell?

◆ Is this then a poem about a fairy story? What do the children think it is about? Look at the line 'shall life inherit'. What sort of life do they think the poet means? (See the note above.)

◆ They may come to the idea about the pilgrimage being a journey of life (and a journey to life). If not, suggest to them that this might be an interpretation of the poem.

◆ Then ask them to think what 'the giants' and 'hobgoblins' could be – are they real creatures, or something else? You could introduce and discuss the fact that the author, Bunyan, wrote elsewhere about the Giant Despair.

◆ Have a second reading, perhaps to end the session: note the masculine language. Tell the children that it is sometimes said or sung using the feminine pronoun. Read the poem again substituting feminine pronoun. Does it make any difference? Why do they think people do it?

◆ Ask the children to illustrate the poem. They could label the giant and hobgoblins with the things that they might symbolize, or simply confine themselves to a literal illustration of it.

Further RE activities

◆ Look at 'dismal stories' in the hymn. How can stories discourage us? Discuss what encourages people to be brave. How can we encourage one another? Discuss how songs can make a difference to how you feel. What sort of songs a) cheer people up, b) make them feel happier or c) make them feel braver?

◆ Learn the hymn tune, if the children don't know it already. Discuss why it might be sung in church. Why might people sing it to themselves at other times?

◆ Ask them to draw either a fictional person's life as a journey, showing the hills and valleys, or their own life. What things have been difficult? What changes have they had? What have been the good things?

◆ Read the biography of John Bunyan, on page 58 of this book.

◆ Read parts of the *Pilgrim's Progress* in a children's version, such as *Pilgrim's Progress* by Geraldine McCaughrean (Hodder Children's Books, 1999).

◆ Discuss bravery in all its different forms. What is needed for different occasions? When have they had to be brave? Raise the issue of being brave enough to have another go when you've had a failure, or how you might have to feel brave in starting at a new school.

◆ Find out about pilgrimages to holy places in different faiths. Also look at walks that are undertaken to raise money for charity or to draw attention to the needs of a community. You might also organize a sponsored event for the school or for a local charity.

◆ Some useful further reading on the theme of bravery: *Two weeks with the Queen* by Morris Gleitzman (Puffin Books, 1989).

Further literacy ideas

◆ Look at some of the linguistic features of the text:
– the pronouns and to whom they refer
– the inversion of sentence. How might they be written in prose?

◆ Find synonyms for some words from the text, for example 'valour', 'constant', 'dismal', 'daunt' and 'fears'.

◆ Make a collection of words for mythical or fairy-tale beings. What sort of feelings or ideas are associated with them?

◆ Look at the way bravery is a common theme in children's stories. Discuss the form of a classic quest story in which someone has to be brave: they set out on a quest; something interferes; they have to overcome it. Ask the children to write their own story.

John Bunyan

PHOTOCOPIABLE

Genre
non-fiction;
biography

John Bunyan was born in Bedford, England in 1628. When he was young he served in the army of Oliver Cromwell, in the English Civil War. One incident during this war made an important difference to Bunyan's life. A friend took his place in a battle and was killed. Bunyan felt afterwards that God must have saved his life for a special purpose.

He was a tinker by trade and had very little schooling. In 1655 his first wife died leaving him with four children to bring up. He was especially devoted to his little daughter who was blind. He had a very strong sense that he was a wicked man, a sinner, though as far as we know his worst faults were a love of dancing on the village green, bell-ringing and sometimes an overwhelming urge to swear. He often felt that he was battling with Satan, the devil.

In 1660 he was arrested for preaching without permission of the church and king. He spent the next twelve years in prison. He helped support his second wife and children by making bootlaces and selling them at the prison door. He was released in 1672 but he went on preaching without permission, and six months later was back in prison. He was not the only one at the time imprisoned for his religious beliefs.

During his time in prison, Bunyan wrote a number of books including the first part of his most famous work, *Pilgrim's Progress*. It sold 100,000 copies in Bunyan's lifetime.

Pilgrim's Progress is an allegory, a story in which a second meaning lies beneath the obvious meaning. It tells the story of Christian who sets out on a journey. It is a hard road with many obstacles. Other travellers, such as Mr Worldly Wiseman, try to persuade him to turn back. Through much of his journey Christian is hampered by a heavy burden, his sins. But he comes to a cross on a hill; and there the burden rolls off his back. He meets the Giant Despair in Doubting Castle, and he passes through the city of Vanity Fair, where the people spend their life in nothing but making money and pleasure activities. At long last he passes through the river of Death where he is greeted by saints and angels.

'The Pilgrim's Hymn' (see page 55) picks up the theme of this story.

John Bunyan

Genre
*non-fiction;
biography*

RE objectives
◆ To learn about a well-known Christian figure.
◆ To look at standing up for your beliefs.

Previous knowledge
This passage will be more interesting if studied together with 'The Pilgrim's Hymn', page 55.

Key words
Allegory.

Discussing the text
◆ Introduce the text as an opportunity to learn more about the author of 'The Pilgrim's Hymn'. Ask the children to suggest things about Bunyan they know or can guess at already from the hymn.

◆ Read the text. Make a joint list of ten things that are learned about John Bunyan (including the reason he went to prison) Draw out, if it doesn't come from the children, that he was a poor man for much of his life. They may need to look up in the dictionary to find out what a tinker was. What religion do they think he belonged to? (The text does not make this explicit.)

◆ Look at the date. How long ago did Bunyan live? What was happening in England at the time of his early life?

◆ Ask the children to suggest what was hard and difficult about John Bunyan's life. When did he need to be brave?

◆ How did he think about himself? Do the children agree that 'a love of dancing on the village green, bell-ringing and sometimes an overwhelming urge to swear' are faults?

◆ Does the author of the text share John Bunyan's view that he lived a wicked life? What do we learn about John Bunyan's book from the text?

◆ Encourage the children to draw scenes from the life of Bunyan.

Further RE activities

◆ Note the idea that Christians don't always agree with one another. Both the church and John Bunyan were Christians, but Bunyan, like many others, did not submit or 'conform' to the authority of the Church of England which had legal authority. Make a list of Nonconformist churches today, for example, Methodists and Baptists, but also look at ecumenical councils, and joint work together through such organizations as Christian Aid.

◆ Look out for newspaper articles about people today who are imprisoned for their beliefs. Tell the children about the work of Amnesty International.

◆ Discuss difficulties in standing up for one's beliefs

◆ Encourage the children's thoughts about Bunyan as a role model. Let them suggest other role models, and give their reasons.

◆ Invite the children's ideas on wickedness. (Take account of recent usage of 'wicked' meaning 'good' in some children's vocabulary.)

Further literacy ideas

◆ This account is written mainly in quite short sentences. Take a series of these and see how they sound if they are linked with conjunctions. Experiment with different ways of linking them up or rewriting them as longer sentences.

◆ Look at the names 'Mr Worldly Wiseman' and 'Giant Despair'. What other characters in fiction do the children know whose name expresses their nature? (For example, Artful Dodger and Superman.)

◆ Find out more about famous allegories. Read a children's version of Animal Farm.

◆ Read biographies of other authors, such as Hans Christian Andersen and Lewis Carroll.

◆ Ask the children to write a brief biography about themselves or about a friend in terms of something they were good at.

Longfellow's Carol

Genre
*poem in
ballad form;
carol*

1. I heard the bells on Christmas Day
   Their old familiar carols play,
   And mild and sweet the words repeat
   Of peace on earth, good will to men.

2. And thought how, as the day had come,
   The belfries of all Christendom
   Had rolled along the unbroken song
   Of peace on earth, good will to men.

3. Till, ringing, singing on its way,
   The world revolved from night to day,
   A voice, a chime, a chant sublime
   Of peace on earth, good will to men.

4. Then from each grim accursed mouth
   The cannon thundered in the South
   And with the sound the carols drowned
   Of peace on earth, good will to men.

5. It was as if an earthquake rent
   The hearth-stones of a continent,
   And made forlorn the households born
   Of peace on earth, good will to men.

6. And in despair I bowed my head;
   "There is no peace on earth," I said;
   "For hate is strong, and mocks the song
   Of peace on earth, good will to men."

7. Then pealed the bells more loud and deep:
   "God is not dead; nor doth he sleep!
   The wrong shall fail, the right prevail,
   With peace on earth, good will to men."

By HW Longfellow, (1807–82), very slightly adapted

About the author

Henry Wadsworth Longfellow was born in 1807 in Portland, Maine, USA. From a very early age he was fascinated by the sounds of words, and by traditional stories and ballads. Perhaps his most famous poem is the long narrative ballad *The Song of Hiawatha*, based on Native American stories. He was deeply concerned with the issue of slavery which led to the American Civil War (1861–65) and wrote a series of poems highlighting the evils of slavery. He died in 1882.

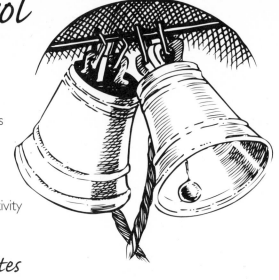

Longfellow's Carol

Genre
poem in ballad form; carol

RE objective

◆ To develop an understanding of the Christmas message of peace and goodwill.

Previous knowledge

The appearance of angels to the shepherds in the nativity story would be useful.

Background notes

This poem was clearly written in the context of the American civil war, with Longfellow voicing the sentiment that many must feel when Christmas takes place against the backdrop of war.

What meaning can these words have when people keep fighting? And yet the poem also expresses forcefully the great Christian hope that right and good will prevail in the end. (Note: the word 'grim' in the fourth verse has been substituted for the original 'black'.)

Key words

Peace; war; goodwill; carol; Christendom.

Discussing the text

◆ Read the title and discuss what a carol is. Its original meaning is a joyful song or dance performed in a circle, usually associated with a festival, especially Christmas. Look at the biographical note on the author and establish the period when the poem was written. Note the layout of a poem or song.

◆ Read the first verse together. Where do the children think the bells were playing? Note the use of 'I'. Longfellow is writing about his experiences, his thoughts. Where do the words 'peace on earth, good will to men' come from?

◆ Read the second and third verses and draw the children's attention to the word 'belfries'. What is Longfellow thinking about? For how long a period is he suggesting these words have been repeated?

◆ Read the fourth to sixth verses. What seems to be happening here? Why is there no peace on earth? Let the children construct a meaning and say where they've got it from. You might make a link here with the biographical note. How is Longfellow feeling?

◆ Look at the final verse. Ask the children for suggestions for the meaning of 'prevail'. What does Longfellow hear in the music of the bells? What does he appear to be feeling? What is he hoping for? What do they think that Longfellow believes?

◆ Read the whole carol, asking the children to reflect in their voices the mood of each verse, looking to be firm at the end. Children might write a percussion accompaniment that reflects the shape of the poem. Review the symbol of bells – how they contrast with the cannon, and how they carry messages.

◆ Illustrate each verse of the poem, choosing colours which seem to reflect the mood of each section.

Further RE activities

◆ Discuss the children's understanding of the Christian message of peace and goodwill at Christmas. What do they make of it? Why do people think about peace at Christmas? What do they think good will means? Ask for examples.

◆ Encourage the children to make Christmas cards which pick up on the theme of peace. Ask them to write their own poem about peace inside the card.

◆ Look in the newspapers for items about war in the world today. Where are people seeking to make peace?

◆ Discuss with the children how they can be peacemakers themselves in school. What do they think are the characteristics of peacemakers? Draw their attention to the Beatitudes in the Bible (Matthew 7: 9 'Blessed are the peacemakers').

◆ Ask the children to find out about organizations which work for peace, for example, the Fellowship of Reconciliation based at Coventry Cathedral, the Corrymeela Community in Northern Ireland, and the work of Archbishop Desmond Tutu.

◆ Compare this carol to other carols the children know and note any similarities and differences.

Further literacy ideas

◆ Make a list of all the words to do with bells and singing.

◆ Look at the rhyming pattern in each verse, especially the internal rhyme in the third line.

◆ Look at the repetition of the final line of each verse. Why do the children think the poet is repeating it?

◆ Take out some of the lines and rewrite them, focusing on the meaning but losing the rhyme and rhythm.

◆ Read other poems or sections of poems by Longfellow. (Note: these are available on the Internet, see the Resources list, page 160.)

A Legend of the Wise Men

Genre
fiction; legend

In Gebas, in Media, a city which lies near the border of the desert, there lived, many, many years ago, three men who were famed for their wisdom.

They were also very poor, which was a most uncommon state of affairs; for, in Gebas, knowledge was held in high esteem, and was well recompensed. With these men, however, it could hardly have been otherwise, for one of them was very old, one was afflicted with leprosy, and the third was an Ethiopian. People regarded the first as much too old to teach them anything; the second they avoided for fear of contagion; and the third they would not listen to because they thought they knew that no wisdom had ever come from Ethiopia.

Meanwhile, the three wise ones became united through their common misery. They begged during the day at the same temple gate, and at night they slept on the same roof. In this way they at least had an opportunity to while away the hours, by meditating upon all the wonderful things which they observed in Nature and in the human race.

One night as they slept side by side on a roof, the eldest among them awoke; and hardly had he cast a glance around him, before he wakened the other two.

"Praised be our poverty, which compels us to sleep in the open!" he said to them. "Awake! and raise your eyes to heaven."

This was a night which no one who witnessed it could ever forget! The skies were so bright that the heavens looked deep and transparent and full of waves, like a sea. The light surged backwards and forwards and the stars swam in their varying depths; some in among the light-waves; others upon the surface.

But farthest away and highest up, the three men saw a faint shadow appear. This shadow travelled through space like a ball, and came nearer and nearer, and, as the ball approached, it began to brighten. But it brightened as roses do when they burst from their buds. It grew bigger and bigger, the dark cover about it turned back by degrees, and light broke forth on its sides into four distinct leaves. Finally, when it had descended to the nearest of the stars, it came to a standstill. Then the dark lobes uncurled themselves back and unfolded leaf upon leaf of beautiful, shimmering, rose-coloured light, until it was perfect, and shone like a star among the stars.

When the poor men beheld this, their wisdom told them that at this moment a mighty king was born on earth: one whose majesty and power should rise higher than any king that had come before; and they said to one another: "Let us go to the father and mother of the new-born babe and tell them what we have seen! Maybe they will reward us with a purse of coin or a bracelet of gold."

They grasped their long travelling staves and went forth. They wandered through the city and out from the city gate; but there they felt doubtful for a moment as they saw before them the great stretch of dry, smooth desert, which human beings dread. Then they saw the new Star cast a narrow stream of light across the desert sand, and they wandered confidently forward with the Star as their guide.

All night long they tramped over the wide sand-plain, and throughout the entire journey they talked about the young, new-born king, whom they should find resting in a cradle of gold, playing with precious stones. They whiled away the hours by talking over how they should approach his father, the king, and his mother, the queen, and tell them that the heavens foretold for their son power and beauty and joy greater than Solomon's. They prided themselves upon the fact that God had called them to see the Star. They said to themselves that the parents of the new-born babe would not reward them with less than twenty purses of gold; perhaps they would give them so much gold that they no longer need suffer the pangs of poverty.

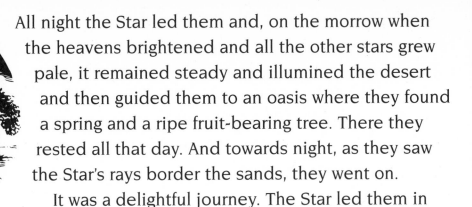

All night the Star led them and, on the morrow when the heavens brightened and all the other stars grew pale, it remained steady and illumined the desert and then guided them to an oasis where they found a spring and a ripe fruit-bearing tree. There they rested all that day. And towards night, as they saw the Star's rays border the sands, they went on.

It was a delightful journey. The Star led them in such a way that they did not have to suffer either hunger or thirst. It led them past the sharp thistles, it avoided the thick, loose, flying sand; they escaped the burning sunshine and the hot desert storms. The three wise men said repeatedly to one another: "God is protecting us and blessing our journey. We are His messengers."

But as they travelled they fell under the power of greed. The star-wanderers' hearts became transformed into as dry a desert as the one which they travelled through. They were filled with pride.

"We are God's messengers!" repeated the three wise ones. "The father of the new-born king will not reward us too well, even if he gives us a caravan laden with gold."

By and by, the Star led them over the far-famed River Jordan, and up among the hills of Judaea. One night it stood still over the little city of Bethlehem, which lay upon a hill-top, and shone among the olive trees.

But the three wise ones looked around for castles and fortified towers and walls, and all the other things that belong to a royal city; but of such they saw nothing. And what was still worse, the Star's light did not even lead them into the city but remained over a grotto near the wayside. There, the soft light stole in through the opening, and revealed to the three wanderers a little Child, who was being lulled to sleep in its mother's arms.

Although the three men saw how the Star's light encircled the Child's head like a crown, they remained standing outside the grotto. They did not enter to prophesy honours and kingdoms for this little One. They turned away without betraying their presence. They fled from the Child, and wandered down the hill again.

"Have we come in search of beggars as poor as ourselves?" they said. "Has God brought us here that we might mock Him, and predict honours for a shepherd's son? This Child will never attain any higher distinction than to tend sheep here in the valley."

The three had not wandered very far before they thought they had gone astray and had not followed the Star rightly.

They turned their gaze upward to find again the Star, and the right road; but then the Star which they had followed all the way from the East had vanished from the heavens.

The three strangers made a quick movement, and their faces expressed deep suffering.

They realized that they had sinned against God.

And it happened with them, just as it happens with the ground in the autumn, when the heavy rains begin to fall. They shook with terror, as one shakes when it thunders, and there is lightning; their whole being softened and humility, like green grass, sprang up in their souls.

For three nights and days they wandered about the country, in quest of the Child whom they would worship; but the Star did not appear to them. They grew more and more bewildered, and suffered the most overwhelming anguish and despair. On the third day they came to a well to drink. And, as they bent over the water , God pardoned their sin. They saw in the well's depths the reflection of the Star which had brought them from the East. Instantly they saw it also in the heavens and it led them again to the grotto in Bethlehem, where they fell upon their knees before the child, and said, "Thou shalt be the greatest king that ever lived on earth from creation until destruction." And they gave him gifts of gold and spices.

Then the Child laid his hand upon their lowered heads, and when they rose, lo! the Child had given them gifts greater than a king could have granted; the old beggar had become young, the leper was made whole, and the Ethiopian's wisdom so shone forth that it was sought after thereafter throughout the world. And it is said of them that they were glorious and that they departed and became kings – each in his own kingdom.

Adapted from 'The Wise Men's Well' in Christ Legends and Other Stories by Selma Lagerlof, translated by Velma Swanston Howard (Floris Books, 1993)

A Legend of the Wise Men

Genre
fiction; legend

RE objectives

◆ To develop awareness of the legends of Christianity.

◆ To provide opportunity for discussion on prejudice.

Previous knowledge

Familiarity with the story of Christmas desirable but not strictly necessary.

Background notes

The Christian story of the wise men's visit to Jesus is found in the New Testament, Matthew 2: 1–12. In this account there is no mention of kings, nothing of their names, nor is a number specified. These are all later embellishments. The Christmas story as it is popularly told is a combination of the nativity story found in Luke and the one found in Matthew with detail that has accrued over time.

The story has led to many other legends. Some, such as the Russian Babushka, are genuine legends, stories passed down over centuries whose original authors have been forgotten. Others are written in the form of legend (for example, 'The Fourth Wise Man' by Henry van Dyke). This story is adapted from one found in a volume *Christ Legends and Other Stories*, but it is unclear whether it originated with the author or was collected during her travels in the Middle East. Selma Lagerlof was a Swede and the first woman to win the Nobel prize for literature. As a child she needed special care, after being struck with infantile paralysis, and grew passionate about stories having been cut off from children's games.

In Lagerlof's telling, the narrator is a personification of Drought. This version has been adapted from it.

The legend picks up and develops the theme that the Christ Child was sought first in the palace, but his kingdom belonged to another place.

Key words

Wise; legend; desert.

Discussing the text

◆ Look first at the title. What does it tell us about what sort of story it is? 'A Legend' implies one story among many. To whom do the children think the 'Wise Men' refers?

◆ Read the whole story to the children, preferably without them looking at the text. It deserves to be read in one sitting uninterrupted as though by a fireside.

◆ Let the children think about the story; quickly recap it and encourage them to make open comment about it. The children may comment on the inconsistency of the wise men suddenly having gifts to offer, and speculate where they come from.

◆ Read the text again, this time with the children. Discuss what prompted the wise men's departure. What did they hope for? What did they receive? Why did they nearly miss out? How does the story tell the reader that this child is no ordinary child, nor even an ordinary king?

◆ Discuss how this story is different from the story of the wise men with which they are familiar from memory. Look at the fact that it is a legend. What makes it read like a legend?

◆ Ask the children to read through the text again, and to draw either their favourite scene or to make a strip cartoon version of it, using the text as a guide.

Further RE activities

◆ Ask the children to write the story as they remember it. Compare the children's accounts of the wise men with the gospel version. Look at other stories of the wise men. Discuss why it is that there are so many different stories, encouraging the children not only to think about the growth of embellishments, but also to see that the nativity is such a central story people revisit it over and over again. Compare this story with Matthew 2: 1–12. Which elements of the gospel story has the writer accepted? Which elements have been omitted and what has been elaborated?

◆ Look at the prejudice of the citizens of Gebas towards the three wise men, and use it to stimulate a discussion on prejudice.

◆ Discuss the concept of wisdom. What makes somebody wise? Is this the same as being clever or knowing a lot?

◆ Discuss the effect of greed on people, but try not to preach. Let the children consider how greed affects people, then ask them to write their own fable about greed.

◆ Using school resources, look for other Christmas legends associated with the wise men, for example Babushka.

Further literacy ideas

◆ In shared reading, read closely the paragraphs describing the sky and the first appearance of the star. What images are conjured in the children's minds? In what way do they see the sky like the sea, or a star like a rose? Give the children photos or paintings of the sky, and ask them to paint it in words.

◆ Draw the children's attention to the metaphors of deserts and green shoots used to describe the state of the wise men's hearts or souls. Ask the children to think of other weather images to describe moods and feelings, for instance whether we would say someone was sunny, or their heart frozen, or talk of raining in heart, or a heart melting like snow.

◆ Look at other linguistic features of the text, for example the use of capital letters for 'Star', 'Child' and 'God'; and at antonyms within the text or implied by it, from old to young, poor to rich, pride to humility, greed to generosity.

◆ Look at the classic structure of a legend: a setting long ago and in an exotic place; talk of kings; a miracle or magic; the symmetry of the story with each character having his problem cured; the quest thwarted and then resolved; and the significance of the number three. Encourage the children to recall other stories where the number three is important.

Hinduism

The sacred writings of Hinduism come in many forms, all written in Sanskrit and all encompassing a considerable period of time. The earliest are probably the hymns and philosophical speculation of the Vedas, dating from the second millennium BC. Much later, from about the 4th century AD, are epics describing the exploits of gods and heroes. Like many scriptures they had their origins in an oral tradition, before being written in generally accepted versions. Amongst these are the best-known and best-loved Hindu scriptures, the Ramayana and the Mahabharata. These scriptures are not drawn together in one revered text.

The scriptures are less central than in religions such as Islam and Sikhism. They are studied and contemplated, particularly the Vedas and the Bhagavad Gita (a section of the Mahabharata), but study of the scriptures is seen as one form of spirituality among many.

The two great epics, and many other Hindu tales, speak of the god Vishnu coming to earth when evil has got the upper hand in the constant struggle between good and evil. In these stories Vishnu has come in both animal and human forms, known as avatars. In the Mahabharata he appears as Krishna, the mischievous boy who becomes the thoughtful warrior. The Ramayana tells the story of King Rama, perhaps the most famous and popular of all the avatars of Vishnu. Whereas the Mahabharata is said to express the entire scope of Hinduism, the Ramayana offers, in the character of Rama, a model for the ideal Hindu life. In his struggles to rescue his queen Sita from the demon Ravana, Rama is seen as an example of honour, strength in the fight against evil, and obedience to social duty. The moral values which Sita upholds are seen as the ideal model of womanhood. For the majority of Hindus, the Ramayana is experienced in drama and dance during festivals such as Diwali, rather than closely studied. Since stories from the Ramayana are readily available in children's versions we have not included them here, but have given children a taste of the personal reaction of one Hindu writer to these traditional stories. We have also given a version of a tale first heard orally in the course of a Hindu childhood, which precedes the Ramayana story in its chronology and points to its themes.

We have also sought to present Hinduism as a truly world faith by contrasting two Hindu temples in different parts of the world, both far distant from India. One of these gives the view of a non-Hindu visitor, the other is written by those involved in the development of the temple and was originally written mainly for Hindus in Britain. These texts also give children the opportunity to compare the perspective of the authors: the difference between writing from the inside of the religion and from the outside.

A Letter from Mombasa

Genre
non-fiction account of events

Likoni Guest House
Mombasa
Kenya
12 March

Dear David and Anne

Well, I've arrived OK here in Africa. Mombasa is very hot and airless, but I've only got a few days to spare for sightseeing before I have to go to Nairobi to start work, so I set off to see as much as possible. I can't tell you about everything, because my brain is reeling with new and strange sights. So I'll just tell you about my visit to the Temple of Shiva. I was a bit surprised to find it listed in my guidebook as one of the places to visit, but apparently there is a large community of Indians in Mombasa. By the time I got there in mid-afternoon, my feet were dusty and swollen, and my head was buzzing with the traffic and car-horns. They just don't seem to stop! I could see the shining white pinnacles of the temple from some distance away, dazzling against the hot blue of the tropical sky, with a gleaming gold statue on the very top, too bright to see what it was.

When I went in the gate, the heat and glare seemed even worse. The Indian community are still building the outer parts of the temple, and everywhere was hard, hot white marble and bare sun-scorched earth. But as I came closer to the central shrine, everything changed. There was a large shady tree with a seat round the

trunk, and under a cool roof with open colonnades down the side, the main part of the temple was built in dark, restful green and white stone. Beyond it I could see a shady courtyard where a few old men and women sat quietly talking and drinking tea. A notice at the entrance welcomed visitors, and asked us to remove our shoes as we entered under the roof.

What a relief to take off my dusty, sticky sandals, and step up onto the smooth, cold marble with my bare feet! It reminded me, David, of that time I stopped you taking off your shoes in the library when you were little. That was a hot day, too, I remember. But here taking off your shoes is a sign of respect for the temple and the god Shiva. In the centre of the shrine was a statue of Nandi, the great Bull of Shiva, carved out of a milky-white, translucent stone. I've never seen an animal look so peaceful, powerful and dignified.

At one end of the temple I could see more pictures and statues, and two large ornate-looking doors stood open. I stepped closer and recognized statues of Hanuman, the monkey god, Ganesha the elephant-headed god, and pictures of the beautiful, beloved god Krishna dancing with the gopis, the young girls who looked after the cows in the village where he grew up. Somebody had left a garland of flowers round the neck of Hanuman. The doors were of moulded silver, with lots of scenes from stories about the god Shiva.

The doors opened onto a room almost like a cave: the floor of the inner shrine was built a metre or two below the level of the doors, and I looked down on a small square room filled with oil lamps, silver and flowers. In the middle was the pillar-shaped lingam, the symbol of the Lord Shiva. An old man and a girl about your age, Anne, were caring for the shrine. The man refilled the oil lamps while the girl prepared a dish of coloured rice and sweet cakes, and scattered marigold petals over it. The cakes looked a bit like the ones that Mrs Kotecha brought round for David's birthday last year, but I don't know if they were the same. The girl was absorbed in what she was doing, and I would have liked to take a photo of her while she didn't know I was watching, but it wouldn't have been polite. I spoke to her in English, and she asked the old man whether I might take some photos. They were both very glad that I was interested in what they were doing, but of course by that time the girl was very self-conscious, looking up at me each time she arranged a marigold petal, so I don't know how well the photos will come out.

After I had thanked them I moved into the tree-lined courtyard and spent a little while enjoying the peace and quiet before I put on my sandals, hat and sunglasses, and ventured back into the hot brightness to walk to the European cathedral — it's really strange being in an African city where so many different cultures meet. But I'll have to tell you more about that some other time. I'll write again when I get to Nairobi.

Lots of love

Mum

X X X

A Letter from Mombasa

Genre
non-fiction
account of
events

RE objectives

◆ To develop understanding of Hindu places of worship.

◆ To reflect on ways of showing respect in religious buildings.

Previous knowledge

Some knowledge of Hinduism and the Hindu gods would be helpful.

Background notes

This text indicated the presence of large Hindu communities in Africa, among people of an Indian background. Africa, as well as Europe, has immigrant communities – a fact sometimes forgotten.

Key words
Temple; Lord Shiva; shrine.

Discussing the text

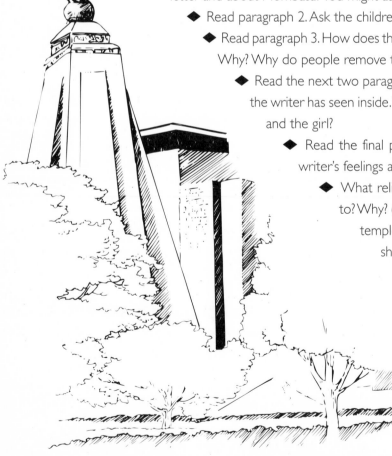

◆ Look at the form of the piece, establishing that it is a letter from a mother to her son and daughter. Ask the children to suggest circumstances in which mothers would write to their children, for example, when they are away on holiday.

◆ Read the first paragraph. What do we learn in the paragraph about the writer of the letter and about Mombasa? You might ask the children to find Mombasa in an atlas.

◆ Read paragraph 2. Ask the children for a description of the temple building.

◆ Read paragraph 3. How does the writer feel when she has taken off her sandals? Why? Why do people remove their sandals when entering a temple?

◆ Read the next two paragraphs and then list with the children everything the writer has seen inside. Why didn't she just take a photo of the old man and the girl?

◆ Read the final paragraph. What do the children think are the writer's feelings about her visit to the city?

◆ What religion do the children think this temple belongs to? Why? (The letter does not mention that this is a Hindu temple.) Children who have already studied Hinduism should recognize the names of the Hindu gods.

◆ How do we know from the letter that there are other religions in Africa?

◆ Read through the letter again. Encourage the children to comment on any aspect of the text which interests or intrigues them – they might talk about a visit they made on holiday to a place of worship.

◆ Encourage the children to use the letter as a source to illustrate a scene from the temple as they would imagine it to be.

Further RE activities

◆ Look in the library or on the Internet for a description of a Hindu temple in India or in Britain and compare it with this temple. What are the similarities and differences?

◆ Ask the children to look for pictures, or you could produce artefacts, of the gods mentioned in the text. How do they fit with what they have imagined and drawn?

◆ Read stories about any of the gods mentioned in the text.

◆ Discuss why it is important to show respect and be polite. What are the customs for showing respect within the children's communities, at home and when going somewhere else? Discuss the fact that different communities have different ways of showing respect.

◆ Children find out about other religions observed in Africa from books about Africa, including any myths and legends.

◆ Ask the children to write a comparison between this place of worship and one they have visited.

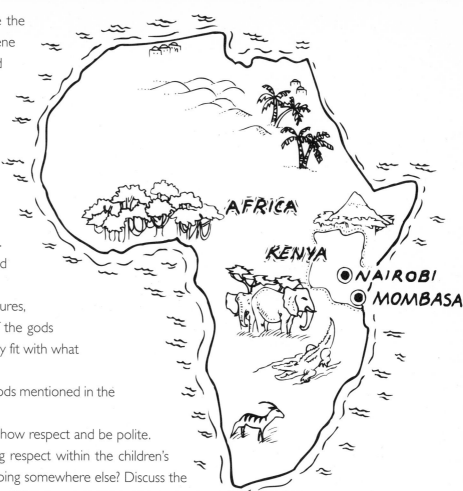

Further literacy ideas

◆ Look for things in the letter that make it personal, and not simply a description that could be found in a travel guide to the building (including the use of the first person singular 'I').

◆ Identify words and phrases that convey the weather and atmosphere of the city.

◆ Find words and phrases that indicate that Mombasa is a city and not some small country town.

◆ Find the words and phrases that convey the atmosphere inside the temple compound.

◆ Ask the children to write a letter describing a place they have visited recently, attempting to convey the atmosphere and not simply what they saw or did.

◆ Children could then use information from the letter to write a description for a guidebook. Encourage them to use an impersonal style.

◆ Ask the children to pretend they are one of the children in the letter and to write a letter in reply, drawing on their own lives.

Monkey Face

From The Monkey God and other Hindu tales by Debjani Chatterjee

PHOTOCOPIABLE

Genre
*fiction;
traditional
tale*

"Narad has always been rather proud, but these days he seems to have quite a swollen head," said Vishnu. "He is boasting a lot and it worries me." Vishnu, the great god who protects all, cares for each and every person. Vishnu liked Narad very much, in spite of all his faults. He knew that Narad was basically a good man who prayed a lot, loved to sing songs about Vishnu and was a jolly companion.

Vishnu's lovely wife, the goddess Lakshmi, was amused. "Well, that's nothing new. He knows he is handsome and has always been vain about his appearance. His vanity is certainly very odd in a holy man. But then Narad is unusual."

Vishnu sighed, "It's not just that. This time I think he has gone too far. He is boasting that he is so good-looking that every woman who sees him falls in love with him straightaway! At the same time he claims not to care about any woman, no matter how beautiful."

Although Narad was dear to them, both Vishnu and Lakshmi agreed that he needed to be taught a lesson. So they decided on a plan.

In an instant Vishnu created a fabulous kingdom. Lakshmi changed herself into a young and beautiful princess. Portraits of the princess were distributed far and wide. Vishnu made quite certain that a portrait reached Narad too.

"The princess is to marry," shouted the town criers and the drummers beat on their drums. "All who wish to wed her must present themselves at the palace in a week's time. She will select the most handsome man for her husband."

As soon as Narad saw the portrait of the princess, he was enchanted by her beauty. He knew that he had to marry her. Even a week seemed too long for him to wait. "O gracious Vishnu," he prayed, "I am already wonderfully good-looking, but please make me even more handsome if that is possible."

Slowly the days dragged by with Narad dreaming about the princess and admiring his appearance in the mirror. He fancied that he grew better-looking each day.

In a week's time Narad arrived at the palace. Many people were already there, kings and princes among them. He joined the queue, feeling very confident that the princess would choose him. He looked around the great hall and concluded that there was no one to compare with him in looks.

A gasp went through the hall when the princess entered it. "How striking she looks," exclaimed someone. "Oh! I hope I am the lucky man she selects," said another. Narad could only marvel in silence at her beauty. "She is so much more beautiful than her portrait," he thought.

The princess held a sweet-smelling flower garland in her hands. She walked past all the men lined up for her inspection. But to Narad's utter surprise and disappointment she gave him just one brief look and walked quickly past him.

"Well, she won't find anyone better," he muttered furiously. But the princess walked up to the man who stood last in the queue and put her garland around his neck.

Narad could not help himself – he strode into the middle of the hall and appealed to everyone. "H... how could she? I... I am certainly the most handsome man there can be. Surely there must be something wrong with her eyesight!" But everyone laughed to hear him, except the princess and the stranger with the garland, who looked at him with pity.

"You fool," said one of the princes. "It is your brain that is clearly at fault. Have you seen yourself in a mirror lately?"

Narad rushed to a mirror that hung on one wall. Horrified, he saw a monkey's face grimacing back at him.

"Poor Narad," said the man with the garland. "Is appearance so important?" Angrily Narad turned around to face him and before his eyes a transformation took place. Instead of the stranger, Narad now saw the radiant face of Vishnu, the blue god. On the very spot where the princess had stood, was now the goddess Lakshmi.

But Narad did not stop to think about what it all meant. He was still in a rage and glared at them both. "So it was you all along," he shouted. "How dare you play such a cruel trick on me." He soundly cursed them both, "Someday you shall be born on earth and will suffer greatly when you are parted from each other. Only a monkey will be able to help you to come together again."

Narad cursed, but the god and goddess smiled at him and each lifted a hand in blessing. The marble palace, the crowd, the fabulous kingdom, all vanished. With them Narad's anger also disappeared. He suddenly understood that everything that had happened had been planned for his own good by a loving god and goddess. He fell to his knees and begged forgiveness, "O Vishnu, what have I done? How could I place such a terrible curse upon you both when you have always showered blessings on me? O Lakshmi, never again will I boast about my looks or speak insultingly of women."

"Do not worry, my friend," said Vishnu, gently lifting him up. "Lakshmi and I will be born on Earth as Rama and Sita to fulfil your curse, but you too will be born as the monkey god, Hanuman, who will be our faithful friend and share our adventures."

Monkey Face

Genre
*fiction;
traditional
tale*

RE objectives

◆ To widen familiarity with the tradition of Hindu storytelling.

◆ To reflect on pride and vanity.

Previous knowledge

None needed, but a knowledge of the story of the Ramayana could make the story more interesting.

Background notes

This story is from Hindu tradition, and recounts an event leading up to the popular story of Rama and Sita. The story is told in the Ramayana and narrated throughout the Hindu year, in particular at Diwali. In the Ramayana, the god Vishnu and goddess Lakshmi come to earth in human form to overcome evil, the demon king Ravana. The monkey god Hanuman is a key figure in the venture. Narad's curse is fulfilled in the pain of the separation between Rama and Sita when Sita is captured by the evil demon. The power of the curse, and with it the implicit caution about care with words, is a recurring theme in religious and folk literature, as is the warning against vanity. Another major theme within the story is that the gods know what is best for humans; thus Narad's anger at having been tricked turns into acceptance.

The final paragraph of the story expresses Hindu belief in reincarnation: Narad will be born again as the monkey god.

In approaching these themes with the children, it is probably best to be very open-ended, allowing them to pick up on the themes (and indeed others they may have noted) rather than impose interpretations on them (see the Introduction, page 6).

This story has been retold here for children from an oral tradition in which the story was passed on by word of mouth. There is no definitive written version.

How you approach this text will depend to some extent on whether the children are familiar with the story of the Ramayana.

Key words

God; goddess; Vishnu; Lakshmi; trick; curse.

Discussing the text

◆ Look at the title of the story, and the title and subtitles of the book from which it comes. Ask the children what sort of literature (genre) they think the book is, just from the title, and what sort of things they might expect in the story. Ask them if they know the names of any Hindu gods and goddesses who might be in the story.

◆ Read through the story together. Review the basic plot with the children, perhaps by asking them for a title for each scene in the story.

◆ You might discuss what vanity is. Why were the god and goddess concerned to teach Narad a lesson?

◆ Ask the children to construct a character profile for each of the main characters, picking out words from the text which support it.

◆ Discuss the ending of the story. Is it sad or happy?

◆ Encourage an open-ended response to the story (some children may be quite critical of the behaviour of the gods) and consider with the children why this story might have been told. What would people be expected to learn from it?

Further RE activities

◆ Link the story with the Ramayana, either by reading it for the first time in one of the many excellent children's versions to be found in libraries, or by recalling it. A fairly brief version is given in *A Tapestry of Tales* (see the Resources list, page 160).

◆ Read the children more stories from *The Monkey God and other Hindu tales* by Debjani Chatterjee.

◆ Discuss with the children the idea that some religions believe in one God and others in many gods. (Although many Hindus see all gods as being manifestations of one God.) Look for pictures and statues depicting the Hindu gods and goddesses, showing how the characters in the story are represented. You could make a display of these.

◆ Encourage discussion of one or more of the themes in the story. What are the children's thoughts about pride and vanity? When is pride good and appropriate? What is the difference between them? How important is beauty and appearance? How do words have the power to hurt or heal? How might tricking people be cruel?

◆ Talk about Narad's trust that the gods had acted for his own good. Discuss this idea in more general terms. How do parents and teachers act for the good of children?

◆ Read or direct the children to the Greek story of Narcissus, which deals with vanity in a very different fashion. Compare the two stories.

Further literacy ideas

◆ Look at the incidents in the story which are features of many traditional tales, for example, supernatural events.

◆ Build a word bank from within the story, and from elsewhere, of words associated with pride and physical appearance.

◆ Look at words in the text which are substitutes for 'said', enhancing it with meaning, for example, 'sighed', 'shouted', 'cursed' and 'muttered'. Ask the children to think of other words that might be used.

◆ Look for the words and phrases that indicate time passing, and move the narrative along, for example, 'as soon as'.

◆ Ask the children to rewrite the story as a play. Discuss with them how the supernatural elements might be performed (for example, by the use of masks).

Writing the Ramayana

by Ranchor Prime

Genre
journal or personal writing with reference to myth

1. I had heard about the wonderful tale of King Rama and his Queen, Sita, many years ago. I knew it was a story of good and evil, of romance and excitement, which has gripped the imagination of people in India and South-East Asia for thousands of years.

2. But it was going to be difficult to rewrite it as a popular book for Channel Four television. The story is so very old: could I make it relevant for people in Britain today?

3. I got hold of a set of volumes in India. They contained the original Sanskrit text along with the direct English translation, stretching altogether to 2200 pages, written in verse form thousands of years ago by the poet Valmiki. I soon found that I need not have worried, since the story has a magic of its own. As I read through the Sanskrit volumes it came alive.

4. People nowadays don't have the time to read 2200 pages so I worked out that the 645 chapters in the original text would have to be condensed to 35 chapters and 160 pages, which would also have to have room for 80 full-colour pictures. I drew up a plan and settled into a routine. Each day I would read about 60 pages then retell them as a single chapter.

5. Soon I found myself being drawn into the story. I was with Rama and Sita in the jungle. When danger threatened I felt fear. When tragedy struck I felt sad. One day I was reading about the argument between Rama and his father, King Dasarath. The argument led to Rama's exile: he was sent to live in the forest for 14 years. There was a particular scene where he went to say goodbye to his mother. Both of them knew they would probably never meet again. It was so sad, and I was so absorbed in it, that I couldn't help myself: I began to cry. I was sitting in a university library in London and a lecturer who happened to be walking past saw me and thought I was in distress.

6. "Are you all right?" he wanted to know. I assured him I had never felt better. Although I was feeling sad, the sadness was very sweet because the story had come alive, and my tears were proof of its power. I felt happy to be so close to Sita and Rama.

7. Another emotional moment came when I read how Rama's father died. The old king had been forced to banish his beloved son Rama. It broke his heart and he woke alone in the night, unable to come to terms with having lost his son. Then he remembered something that had happened long ago when he was a teenager, a young prince out practising his archery in the forest at night. By accident he had shot a boy in the darkness. The boy died in his arms and in deep distress he had gone to find the boy's parents, who lived in the forest and were blind. He told them the dreadful news, and the boy's father cursed him.

8. "You have killed our son and without him to look after us we will die. Because of this cruel act I foretell that you will die without your son." At that moment the aged king, lying alone in his bed in the middle of the night, realized that his fate had returned to haunt him, and in anguish he died from a broken heart.

9. As the weeks went by I moved deeper and deeper into the Ramayana. The evil character of Ravana made his appearance and kidnapped Sita, hiding her away on his island fortress of Lanka, where she was tormented by his demons and goblins. Rama searched everywhere for her in deep distress. One passage stands out in my memory.

10. The poet described the monsoon rains in the deep jungle. How streams gushed down the hillsides, coloured red and yellow by the earth and carrying flowers and leaves washed down from the trees. Birds called through the rain and thunder rumbled as storm clouds gathered against the mountain slopes, deluging the lush green forest. I could feel the wetness and smell the steaming earth. You know that wonderful smell of summer rain on a hot day.

11. Then came the picture of Rama. In the midst of the monsoon storm he sat outside his mountain hideout and his face was wet, not with rain, but with his own tears as he wept for Sita. It was as if the whole world was mourning, the heavens crying, for the loss of the beautiful Sita.

12. Soon after came good news: Rama's faithful servant, the monkey-god Hanuman, had discovered where Sita was. But although she was found he could not rescue her. That would need a full-scale invasion of Lanka and the overthrow of the demon-king Ravana.

13. So the story slowly reached its great climax. (By now I had reached page 1400). Scene after scene swept past. Rama built his famous floating bridge across the ocean to the island of Lanka. Mighty foes did duel to the death, displaying wonderful courage and fighting on the earth and in the sky, using magic powers. The battle for Lanka unfolded, over 600 pages of it, but still the great hero and his arch-enemy did not meet. Although I knew very well how it was all going to end, I was held in suspense as Ravana cheated and deceived his attackers again and again. But all the time his strength and the strength of his armies got less and less. At last came the climax: Rama and Ravana met in a fight to the death. Even this took up over 100 pages and two of my chapters. When the final moment came, and Ravana lay dead, I felt elated and went for a long celebratory walk in the park. I felt as if I had killed him myself!

14. The main story of the Ramayana ends here, with Sita rescued and returning with her beloved Lord Rama to their capital city of Ayodhya. This victorious return is celebrated by Hindus as their most important festival, Diwali, the Festival of Lights, when lamps are lit around every household to welcome Sita and Rama home from exile.

15. But the full Ramayana does not end here. Perhaps it would be too simple and straightforward to have such a predictable happy ending. Or perhaps the truth really was different, and further tragedy struck.

16. It seems that after they returned the couple lived happily in love for two years. Then one day Rama heard that there were some who criticized him for taking back his wife after she had stayed in the household of the demon-king Ravana. They claimed she had been unfaithful to Rama. There are always people in this world who are looking to find fault, especially with their king and queen, and there was no truth in their evil gossip. But when Rama heard these rumours he decided he must ask Sita, although she was expecting his child, to leave the city and live apart from him with the sages of the forest. He believed absolutely that a ruler must live with honour and always set a perfect example to his people, if he were to command loyalty and obedience. So he did this most awful thing: he asked the woman he loved more than anything in the world to leave him. I found this part of the story very difficult. I wanted to feel loyal to Rama too, after having lived with him through over 2000 pages, but I felt he was being cruel to Sita and to his future child. I was deeply puzzled that it had to be this way.

17. But as I carried on to the last, telling the story as I found it, the mist started to clear and I felt I could begin to see more clearly. It is a strange world we live in, where life is never easy, even if you are a king like Rama. We must all accept things we do not want in life, and learn to live without the things we would like to have. It is hard to understand, but if we have faith that God loves us we will see that all is for the best in the end. At least this is my belief, and the belief of millions who revere Rama as God and Sita as the divine Mother of Mercy.

18. It is this realism that I think makes the Ramayana such a great and lasting masterpiece. It is not just a happy tale of good conquering evil. It is about the trials and difficulties of life on earth, and it also is about honour, courage and duty. And at its heart is the message that above all else, love wins out in the end.

Writing the Ramayana

Genre
journal or personal writing with reference to myth

RE objective

◆ To extend understanding of the Hindu epic, the Ramayana, by seeing how one person has responded to it.

Previous knowledge

None needed.

Background notes

The core story of the Hindu epic, the Ramayana, will be familiar to many children who have heard the tale of Rama and Sita during their studies on Diwali. This moving account of writing a version of the epic for a Channel Four book to accompany a television series makes reference to the story, but it does not depend on knowledge of it. As with a good book review it may spur the children on to reading a version of the epic for themselves, although the structure of the epic is also given in the text.

This is a text which, like many, invites wondering. Some questions about it may be bluntly put, but a tone of wonder in your voice as you share the account with the children may help them enter the spirit of the writing.

Key words

Ramayana; author; Rama; Sita; tragedy.

Discussing the text

◆ The text divides very readily into two or three sessions if it feels too complex to read in one sitting in the context of the literacy hour.

◆ Setting the scene: wonder with the children about the title. If they don't have the knowledge to unravel the meaning of the title, leave it and let them discover the meaning in the reading of the text.

◆ If they are familiar with the core story of the Ramayana, prompt them to remember what they can about it.

◆ Read paragraphs 1–4: the title and the first four paragraphs set the scene for the author's encounter with the story. We learn from them about the task before him and some basic information about the epic.

◆ What job has the author been given? What do we learn about the book that he is rewriting? For whom will he be writing this new version? What is he worried about? How does he set about doing his task?

◆ Read paragraphs 5 and 6 and wonder with the children about what the author means when he writes 'I was with Rama and Sita in the jungle'. Pick up on the emotions he expresses by looking both at the emotive words and the anecdote about the incident in the library.

◆ Ask the children for a chapter title for the section of the epic described in paragraphs 5 and 6, for example, 'Rama is sent into exile'.

◆ Read paragraphs 7–14 quickly with the children, again focusing on the author's response to the text and how he conveys it. You may need to clarify who 'the poet' is in paragraph 10.

◆ Then, perhaps, review the story as it has unravelled.

◆ Have an open-ended discussion encouraging the children to talk and perhaps write about stories which have deeply moved them and/or stories which have enabled them to identify with the main characters.

◆ Review the account, including the story, and then read the final section (paragraphs 14 to 18) which raises a problem the author has with the story and the meaning he makes of it.

◆ Clarify that the children have understood the narrative and why the author is disturbed by it. How does he convey his concern?

◆ Look then at the meaning the author makes of the story.

◆ Discuss what sort of trials and difficulties people face on earth. What do children understand by the terms 'honour, courage and duty'?

◆ Encourage them to reflect on the author's thoughts in the same sort of mood.

Further RE activities

◆ Learn more about how the story is remembered and re-enacted throughout the Hindu year, particularly at Diwali. Look at the Hindu teaching that Rama and Sita were the god Vishnu and his consort Lakshmi come to earth in human form in order to fight evil.

◆ Look again at paragraphs 17 and 18. The author expresses beliefs about the world and about human life. What are these beliefs? Do the children share them? Encourage the children to express agreement and disagreement, satisfaction or dissatisfaction with the author's views.

◆ The story tells of the conquest of evil by fighting. Gandhi, the Hindu pacifist, held this story very dear, but believed that evil could be overcome by non-violent means. Discuss with children the problems of using violence, and look at other ways evil and wrongs in society can be overcome. Let them research more about Gandhi.

◆ Read 'Monkey Face' (page 78) and discuss the connection between the two stories. Does either of them make one feel different about the other?

◆ Read a children's version of the Ramayana. Perhaps explore this further with art and role-play.

◆ Encourage the children to talk and write about a story which has moved them.

Further literacy ideas

◆ Look at features of personal writing found in the text, for example, use of the first person, affective words, expression of opinion and reflection, the author's identification with the characters in the story.

◆ Discuss the metaphor 'the mist started to clear' in paragraph 17 and identify other metaphors and sayings to do with light and dark (not just those found in the story). Link this to the use of lights at Diwali, symbolizing both the welcome home and the theme in the story of good overcoming evil.

◆ Look at the description of the forest and the words used to convey wetness in paragraphs 10 and 11. Contrast this with language which might be used to describe the sort of rain children experience locally.

◆ 'Honour', courage' and 'duty' are all words used to convey morality and virtue. Discuss their meaning with the children. Find other stories which convey virtues and ask children to think of other virtues.

◆ Ask the children to write their own version of a familiar myth or fairy tale which has moved them.

Tividale Tirumala
A Dream in the Making

Genre
information –
public
information
from the
Internet

A Project for the Millennium

The very first Temple in Europe for Lord Venkateswara (Balaji) is currently being built at Tividale near Birmingham, in the centre of England.

Planning permission was obtained from the Black Country Development Corporation for construction on a 12.5 acre (5 hectare) site, and the foundation was laid amidst much celebration on 24 May 1997. Full construction began on 23 February 1998 and has completed the first phase of construction. Artisans from India are now completing the Temple with sacred stone sculptures and decorations. Grand opening ceremonies have taken place for the Sri Ganapathi and Sri Subramanya Swami Temples. In addition on 9 April, the main Temple building was opened. There was a great ceremony for this event involving the installation of Balaji and Hunuman Utsava Moorthries.

Traditional Design

The Temple is being constructed to the highest standards according to our Agama Sastras in a traditional yet unique style based on the shrine at Tirupathi, Andhra Pradesh, India. It will be set amidst landscaped gardens.

The Deities

Lord Balaji, a representation of Shri Vishnu and Lord for the Kaliyuga, will rest in the inner recess of the Temple – the Garbha Gruha (Sanctum). To the right will be the Sannidhi of Shri Mahalakshmi (Goddess of Wealth) seated on eight lotus petals, also known as Padmavathi. There are also plans for shrines for the main prayer hall for Shri Hanuman, the Goddess Kannaka Parameswari and Lord Rama.

Serving the Community

We believe we have a lot to offer the local community: a meeting place open to all, a landmark of beauty and recreational facility in the region to be proud of, local employment and trade, and a base for voluntary work for the needy.

The community centre, which like the Temple will be built in traditional style, will cater for the cultural and social needs of the community at large. Eventually there may be a library and facilities for study and research.

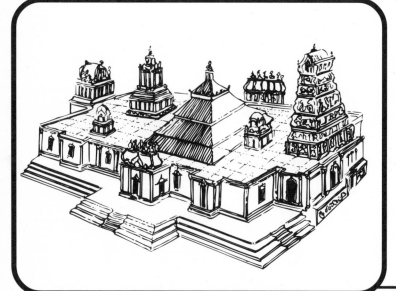

For over ten years the Balaji Temple has been running an annual residential camp for young people, where they can learn about the beauty and depth of their spiritual heritage and its application in the world they live in. The Temple will be a centre of music, arts, philosophy, scriptural learning as well as a place of worship. In this way we will impart our traditions to our children.

A Lasting Monument

We intend the Shri Venkateswara Temple to be a lasting monument to Hinduism and a gift to generations to come. We welcome everyone to visit our Temple site and invite you to join us in our vision.

To find out more contact the Temple office:

Shri Venkateswara (Balaji) Temple of the United Kingdom, off Dudley Road East, Tividale, Oldbury, West Midlands, B69 3DU, England Tel: 0121 544 2256 (international +44 121 544 2256) Fax: 0121 544 2257 (international +44 121 544 2257) – Registered Charity No.326712

From the website www.venkateswara.org.uk, December 1999

Tividale Tirumala A Dream in the Making

Genre
information –
public
information
from the
Internet

RE objectives

◆ To learn about a Hindu Temple in Britain.

◆ To recognize the desire of a community for their own religious building.

Previous knowledge

Some knowledge of Hindu temples and Hindu gods would be useful.

Background notes

There are very few purpose-built Hindu temples in Britain, the majority of buildings where Hindus meet will have been converted from other uses. This text gives a hint as to how the building of temples is an ongoing project which takes time, money and dedication to bring into being.

The deity Shri Venkateswara, an incarnation of Vishnu, is also known as Balaji in the northern parts of India. 'Shri' is usually translated as 'Lord'. Within the temple there are also shrines to other deities.

This text would work best as part of a project on Hinduism.

You will need dictionaries.

Key words

Temple; shrine; community; spiritual heritage.

Discussing the text

◆ Begin with the title. Where does the text come from? What do the children think it is about? Ask them about other millennium projects of which they have heard.

◆ You will probably need to introduce the text as one about a Hindu temple. Have dictionaries on hand so that there can be a race to look up the words 'artisan' and 'deities' once the children have guessed from the context what they might mean.

◆ Look at the title for information as to what the text is about. Wonder with the children about the subtitle 'A Dream in the Making'. Return to this, if necessary, when you have finished reading the text.

◆ Look at the headings for the information that can be found about the temple.

◆ Read through the extract with the children and then brainstorm with them a list of things they have learned about the temple from the text.

◆ Do they think the authors are Hindus themselves or non-Hindus writing about the temple? Why? Identify those items which the authors take for granted the reader will understand (such as Agama Sastra). What does this suggest about who they think will be interested in the temple?

◆ How do we know from the text that, at the time of writing, the temple has been started but that the project is not yet completed? Which things still need doing?

◆ What sort of place do the builders of the temple hope it will be?

◆ Would the children like to visit the temple, and if so, why?

◆ Ask the children to make a poster advertising the temple based on the text.

Further RE activities

◆ Compare the description of the temple here with the description of the temple visited in Mombasa (see page 73).

◆ Visit a local Hindu temple and identify any similarities and differences between it and this site.

◆ Listen to a tape of music that might be sung in the temple.

◆ Find out more about shrines, deities and the format of Hindu worship, possibly presenting the information as 'further information' screens on the website.

◆ Look at the fact that Hindus have images in their places of worship, unlike Islam and Judaism.

◆ Go to the website to see what is currently happening at the temple. See if there is information about other temples on the Internet.

◆ Discuss the idea of places of worship. Why do the children think people want their places of worship to be beautiful and made with the very best materials? Encourage them to talk about buildings they think are beautiful.

Further literacy ideas

◆ Identify words which convey the writer's feelings and hopes about the project, for example 'lasting monument'.

◆ Ask the children to write a list of questions about the temple which are answered by the text, for example, 'Which goddesses have shrines in the temple?' Then write a list of questions prompted by the text but which are not answered within it, for example, 'Who is paying for the temple?' 'Who is Lord Rama?'

◆ Discuss the use of the past, present and future tenses in the text (children could circle each one in different colours), focusing especially on the fact that the present indicates that which is now the case, whereas the future tense is an expression of hope.

◆ Look at the layout, noting that it is based on the printout of a website. How would it have looked on the screen?

◆ Ask the children to pick out words or phrases which they would make 'interactive' to retrieve further information or link to other pages if they were designing this website.

◆ Encourage the children to imagine they are a visitor to the temple when it is completed. They could either design a postcard that could be on sale and write a message on the back, or they could write a longer letter to a friend or a travel guide about it.

◆ Ask the children to design a similar website for an imaginary dream project of their own.

Judaism

At the heart of Judaism lies the Torah, five texts gathered as one, which tell of the origins of the world (see the text on Genesis 1), the establishment of a special relationship between the almighty God and Abraham and his descendants, and the gift of law and land to those descendants after they escaped from slavery in Egypt to return to the land of Israel.

The Torah is studied in Jewish schools and it is also read in the synagogue in the weekly Sabbath services from the beginning to end in a yearly cycle. A young man (and in some traditions of Judaism, a young woman) takes his place as an adult in the congregation by reading from the Torah in the Synagogue services. Copies of the Torah are still scrupulously copied by hand on to a scroll. The scrolls are kept in highly decorated covers, and are not touched by hand. A pointer is used in order to follow the Hebrew lettering which reads from right to left.

For many religious Jews the Torah contains literal truth in all matters, including its account of history; for others it is a book speaking the truth about God and his relationship with Israel. For the former it is also a matter of belief that the Torah was written during the time of Moses, about 1400BC. Those who accept modern scholarship place it around 500BC and regard it as drawing together earlier traditions. Above all, the Torah contains the law, or the word of God, by which the modern religious Jew seeks to live out in his or her life.

The Torah was not the only book of Ancient Israel. There were also the histories, prophecies, love poetry and the psalms, the hymns of temple and synagogue, of which we have included one.

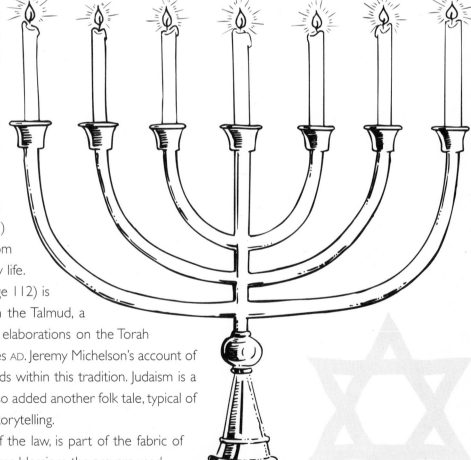

These books, with the Torah itself, constitute the Hebrew Bible, and are also part of the Christian scriptures (see page 40).

The rules for fastening the mezuzah to the door (page 107) exemplify the way that words from the Torah are applied in everyday life. 'The Dog and the Cat' story (page 112) is typical of a creation story from the Talmud, a collection of interpretations and elaborations on the Torah dating from the first four centuries AD. Jeremy Michelson's account of what the law means to him stands within this tradition. Judaism is a faith rich in story, and we have also added another folk tale, typical of the ongoing Jewish tradition of storytelling.

Prayer, as well as fulfilment of the law, is part of the fabric of daily life, and we have included some blessings, the prayers used by Jews in countless everyday situations to acknowledge God's constant care.

In the Beginning

Genre
poetry

In the beginning God created the heavens and the earth.

The earth had no shape; it had no form.

Darkness was upon the face of the deep; and the Spirit of God hovered over the face of the waters.

God said, "Let there be light"; and there was light.

God saw that the light was good; and God separated the light from the darkness.

God called the light Day, and the darkness he called Night. And there was evening and there was morning, one day.

God said, "Let there be a dome in the midst of the waters, and let it separate the waters from the waters."

God made the dome and separated the waters which were under the dome from the waters which were above the firmament.

It was so.

And God called the dome Heaven. And there was evening and there was morning, a second day.

God said, "Let the waters under the heavens be gathered together into one place, and let the dry land be seen."

It was so.

God called the dry land Earth, and the gathering waters he called Seas.

God saw that it was good.

And God said, "Let the earth sprout vegetation, plants bringing seed and fruit trees bearing fruit in which is their seed, each according to its kind, upon the earth."

And it was so.

The earth brought forth vegetation, plants yielding seed according to their own kinds, and trees bearing fruit in which is their seed, each according to its kind.

God saw that it was good.

And there was evening and there was morning, a third day.

God said, "Let there be lights in the dome of the heavens to separate the day from the night; and let them be for signs for seasons, for days and years, and let them be lights in the dome of the heavens to give light upon the earth." And it was so.

God made the two great lights, the greater light to rule the day, and the lesser light to rule the night; he made the stars also.

God set them in the dome of the heavens to give light upon the earth, to rule over the day and over the night, and to separate the light from the darkness. And God saw that it was good.

And there was evening and there was morning, a fourth day.

And God said, "Let the waters bring forth swarms of living creatures, and let birds fly above the earth across the dome of the heavens."

God created the great sea monsters and every living creature that moves, with which the waters swarm, according to their kinds, and every winged bird according to its kind.

God saw that it was good.

And God blessed them, saying, "Be fruitful and multiply and fill the waters in the seas, and let birds multiply on the earth."

And there was evening and there was morning, a fifth day.

And God said, "Let the earth bring forth living creatures according to their kinds: cattle and creeping things and beasts of the earth according to their kinds."

And it was so.

God made the creatures of the earth according to their kinds and the cattle according to their kinds, and everything that creeps upon the ground according to its kind. And God saw that it was good.

Then God said, "Let us make man in our image, after our likeness. Let them have dominion over the fish of the sea, and over the birds of the air, and over the cattle, and over all the earth, and over every creeping thing that creeps upon the earth."

God created man in his own image, in the image of God he created him; male and female he created them.

And God blessed them, and God said to them, "Be fruitful and multiply, and fill the earth and subdue it; and have dominion over the fish of the sea and over the birds of the air and over every living thing that moves upon the earth."

And God said, "Behold, I give you every plant yielding seed which is upon the face of all the earth, and every tree with seed in its fruit; you shall have them for food.

And also to all the living things on the earth, and to every bird of the air, and to everything that creeps on the earth, everything that has the breath of life, I give every green plant for eating."

And it was so.

And God saw everything that he had made, and behold, it was exceedingly good. And there was evening and there was morning, a sixth day.

Chapter 2

Thus the heavens and the earth were finished, and all that was within them.

And on the seventh day God finished his work which he had done, and he rested on the seventh day from all his work which he had done.

So God blessed the seventh day and hallowed it, because on it God rested from all his work, all his work in creating.

Adapted from Fox's Translation of the Torah

In the Beginning

Genre
poetry

RE objectives
◆ To become familiar with and respond to the Judaeo-Christian story of creation.
◆ To become familiar with elements of Judaism and Christianity.

Previous knowledge
None needed, but some knowledge of Christianity and Judaism might be useful.

Background notes
For some Jews and Christians, this story of creation, opening the Torah and the Old Testament, is a literal account revealed to Moses of all that happened at the beginning of all things. For others it is a magnificent piece of poetry, written by the compositors of the Torah who wove together early texts in about the 5th century BC. It sets the scene of God's relationship with the earth and, in particular, with humanity. It proclaims that this earth is good, and God is its creator.

It recounts the creation of man and woman as equal partners. Later, in Chapter 2, there appears a second story which puts the creation of man before woman. There are a number of theories about this second story, but this is not the place to delve into them. In this first account, man and woman stand equal before God, both made in God's likeness.

One of the critical understandings that Key Stage 2 children need to make is that texts may speak something true without being literally true. We do not know quite what the original author believed; we can see that the text reflects the intuitive perception of the time of its writing. The heavens are a dome, the sea stretches beyond dry land to the beyond. We also know that it reflects the conviction that creation is good.

The text also speaks of the hallowing of the seventh day, the Sabbath. Jews are exhorted to rest on the Sabbath in imitation of God who rested on the Sabbath.

This version of the text is based on Jewish and Christian translations. 'Dome' is closer to the Hebrew than the traditional translation of 'firmament'. 'Hover' is a metaphor for God's spirit (or, in another translation, rushing wind) who is like a bird hovering above the water.

For some Christians, the idea of humanity having dominion over the earth implies the right to exploitation of its resources. For the majority of Jews and Christians it is a statement that humanity can use the earth's resources but care must also be taken. We are stewards of creation; it is given to us in trust.

Key words
Creation; good; blessed.

Discussing the text
◆ If you are studying the story in the context of other creation stories, show the children both a Bible and a Torah facsimile – here is a text that belongs to both, and opens both books.
◆ Look at the overall layout of the text. What does it look like? Is it a history or a poem?
◆ Read the text to and with the children.

◆ Read it again, but this time 'orchestrate' it by, for example, having the whole class read the lines that are repeated ('it was so', 'it was good'), and choosing a narrator for the rest.

◆ Look at the use of the word 'dome'. Why use this word about the skies? When do they think the text was written? Why? Did people think differently then? (We might, of course, write about the sky as a dome today.)

◆ If the children raise the question about the clash with scientific accounts, tell them that some Jews and Christians believe it is absolutely true, others believe that it might be true in other ways without telling the scientific story. Encourage the children to discuss that idea.

◆ Possibly as another short session in its own right, look at the idea of man and woman being created in the likeness of God. What do the children think that means? In what ways can you be like someone without being physically the same?

Further RE activities

◆ Discuss the attitude to the earth. Ask the children to suggest things that are good about the world and consider how we can take responsibility for it. Look at the ways humanity has not taken care of it. Develop this further into environmental work, or simply have the children talk and write about how they can take care of the world around them. How can they help create a good place?

◆ Encourage the children to talk and write about something they made which they were pleased with. How did they feel?

◆ Encourage the children to learn more about the Sabbath and Rosh Hashanah, the 'birthday of the world'.

◆ Look at creation stories from other religions, noting any similarities and differences in their themes and attitudes.

◆ Look more closely at the way God is represented, and the use of metaphor (for example, 'the Spirit of God hovered over the face of the waters' – God is like a hovering bird, or a rushing wind). What else is God like, in the text, or in other descriptions the children know?

Further literacy ideas

◆ Carry out more work on metaphors and similes, perhaps linking it with the final point above. Ask the children to think what animals they are like. What other metaphors do we use to describe abstract ideas, such as power, love and fear?

◆ Compare this version with any version of the Bible you have in school.

◆ Look at the list of the following words that are used in different translations. See if the children can spot where they might be substituted in this text. Then ask the children to suggest other synonyms:

beast

sea-serpents

moved across

fowl

herd

animals

living creatures

◆ Read and make a collection of poems that celebrate creation.

◆ In art, ask the children to make little creation books, or copy the text and draw a border that encompasses the seven days. They might make huge displays leading from one day to the next.

◆ As a class, compose an accompaniment to the passage.

◆ Explore further the idea of species.

Psalm 148: A Hymn of Praise

Genre
poetry; hymns

Alleluia
Praise God from the heavens,
praise him in the heights,
praise him, all his angels,
praise him, all ye host.

Praise him, Sun and Moon,
praise him, all shining stars
praise him, highest heavens,
praise him, waters above the heavens,

Let them all praise the name of God
at whose commands they were made;
he established them for ever and ever
by an unchanging decree.

Praise God from the earth,
sea monsters and all the depths,
fire and hail, snow and mist,
storm – winds that obey his word,

mountains and every hill,
orchards and every cedar,
wild animals and all cattle,
reptiles and winged birds,

kings of the earth and all nations,
princes and all judges on the earth,
young men and girls,
old people and children together.

Let them praise the name of God,
for his name alone is sublime
his splendour transcends the strength of his people,
to the praise of all his faithful,
the children of Israel, the people close to him.

Translation adapted from The Jerusalem Bible

Psalm 148: A Hymn of Praise

Genre
Poetry;
hymns.

RE objectives

◆ To develop understanding of Jewish and Christian beliefs about creation.

◆ To encourage attitudes of thankfulness.

Previous knowledge

None necessary, although it would be useful to have done some work on the synagogue.

Background notes

This text can be studied alongside the hymns of praise from Christianity (page 44) and Sikhism (page 147); all three hymns link God with creation, albeit with different focuses. Each one could be studied on a separate day in sequence. The Psalm is a song of the ancient Hebrews, sung now by both Jews and Christians in synagogue and church. It probably would have been accompanied in ancient times by instruments such as the lyre, flute, harp and cymbals.

Key words

Praise; synagogue.

Discussing the text

◆ Perhaps introduce the text by talking about praise. When do teachers praise children? Why do people praise one another? Is it good to receive praise?

◆ Read through the Psalm once. Where do the children think this poem might be said or sung and why? (Some may say in church, in which case tell them it is also sung or said in the synagogue.) Ask the children what else they know about the synagogue.

◆ Return to the Psalm, perhaps reading it again. Who is being asked to praise God? (The word 'host' originally meant 'army' but is also used to mean 'a large number'.) Make a list of all things called on to praise God.

◆ Look at the third verse. Who does it say made everything? What did he use to make them? Focus on the term 'command'; discuss what a command is (a form of speech). Then check that the children understand the meaning of 'decree', and see its connection with 'command'.

◆ In the last verse, check the meanings of 'sublime' and 'transcend', asking a child to read out the dictionary meaning, and then asking the children to suggest what they think the verse means.

◆ Note that 'children of Israel' refers to people who are descendants from Jacob, the ancient Hebrew Patriarch whose name was changed to Israel.

◆ Ask the children to suggest how the hymn should be read: when would they use soft and louder voices, when would they go slower, when quicker. How could they show this on the text?

◆ Suggest the children make up an instrumental accompaniment, possibly just using their body as an instrument. Read through the text with the accompaniment.

◆ Encourage the children to copy the text and illustrate each verse – perhaps with groups taking a verse each if you wanted to make a large frieze.

Further RE activities

◆ Read the creation story as told in Genesis Chapter 1. Compare the beliefs and the order of creation with Psalm 148, and the concept in both that God creates with his word. Introduce and/or develop the idea that although there are some Jews and Christians who believe in a literal six-day creation, others see the creation story as a poem expressing the majesty of the creator, God (see the Background notes on page 97 for further guidance).

◆ Learn more about the synagogue, and the role of singing and music in Jewish worship, both in the synagogue and at home.

◆ Read some other psalms, either with a similar theme of praise, such as Psalms 66 or 105, or a different character, such as Psalms 42, 46 or 77.

◆ Compare this psalm with the hymns of praise from Christianity (page 44) and Sikhism (page 147). Look specifically at the different ways the natural world is invoked in each. The psalm calls on the whole of the world, everything that is in it, to praise God. It is only in the third verse that we have mention of the reason – God created them with his command, that is, by his word.

◆ Discuss whether all people who feel awe in the presence of something beautiful or intriguing always believe in God (this would need to be a very open discussion).

◆ Invite the children to write their own hymn of praise (it doesn't have to be directed at God; it could be towards a parent or friend).

◆ See also the activities suggested in relation to the other hymns of praise from Christianity (page 44) and Sikhism (page 147).

Further literacy ideas

◆ Look at the imperative form of the word 'praise' and its links to command. Is the author asking or telling someone to praise? How would it change the meaning or feeling of the Psalm if the writer had written, 'please praise'. Ask the children to suggest other ways of expressing the imperative, and place them in order from the most forceful to the least.

◆ Look at the use of repetition in all three songs. Ask the children to suggest why repetition is used.

A Selection of Jewish Blessings

Genre
poetry; prayers

For bread
Blessed are you, Lord our G_d, King of the Universe, who brings forth food out of the earth.

For cake and pastry
Blessed are you, Lord our G_d, King of the Universe, who creates different kinds of food.

For fruit which grows on trees
Blessed are you, Lord our G_d, King of the Universe, who creates the fruit of the tree.

For vegetables
Blessed are you, Lord our G_d, King of the Universe, who creates the fruit of the earth.

For all other food
Blessed are you, Lord our G_d, King of the Universe, by whose word all things exist.

On smelling flowers
Blessed are you, Lord our G_d, King of the Universe, who creates fragrant plants.

On smelling spices
Blessed are you, Lord our G_d, King of the Universe, who creates different kinds of spices.

On seeing the wonders of nature
Blessed are you, Lord our G_d, King of the Universe, who performs the work of creation.

On hearing thunder
Blessed are you, Lord our G_d, King of the Universe, whose strength and power fill the world.

On seeing the sea
Blessed are you, Lord our G_d, King of the Universe, who made the great sea.

On seeing a rainbow
Blessed are you, Lord our G_d, King of the Universe, who remembers his covenant and is faithful to it, and keeps his promise.

On seeing the beauties of nature

Blessed are you, Lord our G_d, King of the Universe, who has such as these in His world.

On seeing trees in blossom for the first time in the year

Blessed are you, Lord our G_d, King of the Universe, who has not made His world lack for anything, and has created in it fine creatures and trees to give pleasure to mankind.

On hearing bad news

Blessed are you, Lord our G_d, King of the Universe, the true Judge.

On hearing news good for you and for others

Blessed are you, Lord our G_d, King of the Universe, who is good and does good.

On seeing one who has recovered from serious illness

Blessed are you, Lord our G_d, King of the Universe, who has restored you to us and not to the dust.

On tasting new fruits, on moving into a new home and on using new clothes

Blessed are you, Lord our G_d, King of the Universe, who has kept us alive and supported us and brought us to this season.

On seeing people of unusual appearance

Blessed are you, Lord our G_d, King of the Universe, who varies the forms of creation.

On seeing kings and rulers

Blessed are you, Lord our G_d, King of the Universe, who has given His glory to flesh and blood.

On seeing people with religious knowledge and wisdom

Blessed are you, Lord our G_d, King of the Universe, who has given a share of His wisdom to those in awe of Him.

On seeing people with great secular learning

Blessed are you, Lord our G_d, King of the Universe, Who has given His wisdom to flesh and blood.

TEACHERS' NOTES

A Selection of Jewish Blessings

Genre
poetry; prayers

RE objectives

◆ To develop understanding of Jewish prayer and daily life.

◆ To encourage attitudes of thankfulness.

Previous knowledge

Some knowledge of Judaism and the Jewish Law is helpful.

Background notes

Within Judaism there is a strong theme of remembering God in every aspect of life: wearing a head-covering of some sort, for example, is understood by many Jews to be a constant reminder that human beings are always in the presence of God and are lower than him. Prayers, particularly blessings, are woven into the fabric of life, encouraging an attitude of thankfulness. Thus, in these examples, we find blessings connected to food, nature and people (see also the section on the mezuzah, page 107). These prayers are not requests to make an item holy; they are a recognition that God's holiness, goodness and grace are expressed in the food, in the flowers, in the diversity within the world. They are statements about God, not commands.

The vowel has been omitted from G_d in deference to the custom of many Jews who do not write the holy name even in English.

The word 'blessed' is used in many different ways in different contexts. Its three main meanings are 'happy' or 'fortunate' (usually used of people), 'consecrated' or 'made holy' (usually used of objects), and 'worthy to be reverenced' (used, as here, in relation to God). These different usages are probably too complicated for children of this age, but may need discussion if the children raise different understandings of the word. The strategy suggested in 'Discussing the text' will probably be sufficient.

According to the Jewish Catalog, these blessings date from 400–300BC. If an action is involved (for example, eating bread), the action should immediately follow the blessing.

We have retained the gender bias of the original text.

Clearly, the length and timing of the opening section will depend on whether children have had any studies on Judaism.

Key words

Blessed; universe; king.

Discussing the text

◆ Ask the children to look at the title and then skim through these blessings. Which religion do they come from? Discuss briefly what they remember about the practice and stories of this religion.

◆ What do they notice about the words in these blessings? Draw out that the first words are always the same, and that the vowel is missed out from G_d (see the explanation above). Note that there is a variety of practice used.

◆ Discuss the meaning of the opening words. They express the Jewish belief (shared by Christians and Muslims) in God as the king of all that there is, and state that he is blessed, or good. Ask the children to consider how God is like a king, drawing out that this is a metaphor, expressing that he is in charge.

◆ Look at the link between the headings in bold and the words of the blessings. These are words said for these occasions. Lead into why people might especially think about God being good at these particular times.

◆ Select some or all of these blessings to 'unwrap' individually. You could begin each discussion by encouraging the children to conjure up the sights, smells and feelings associated with each one. You might use simple guided fantasies for some (for example, 'Close your eyes and imagine that you are seeing the sea – the waves might be rolling high, breaking into fountains of spray on the rocks, or they might be calm and still, the moon shining down spreading light across the grey water'). For others, you might use simple prompts, such as: 'I wonder why thunder would be a reminder of God's power?' or 'Why is the rainbow a reminder of a promise or covenant God made?' (See the story of Noah in Genesis 6–8: the rainbow is a sign of God's promise not to flood the world again.)

◆ Look at two blessings: one for religious learning, one for secular. What do the children think 'secular' means? (Non-religious.) Ask the children to suggest subjects of secular learning, for example, the history of England, maths, biology. Why might these be things to be thankful for?

◆ Ask for any other comment on the text, perhaps prompting a discussion on the gender bias. Ask the class to suggest other words which could be used for 'mankind' or 'king'.

◆ Encourage the children to suggest other things for which we can be thankful. What would they add to the list? They could write these down.

Further RE activities

◆ Look at the language about God, pointing out that 'King of the Universe' is one metaphor. Which other words are used about God? (For example, 'shepherd', 'judge' and 'father'.) Although the word 'creator' is not used, God is seen as the creator in these prayers. What other images of God are used in the prayers? What else does God do? (For example keeps us alive.) Look at the way Judaism uses different word images for God, but will not allow pictures of him. Don't stifle any comment on the male bias of much of the language which reflects the views of when it was written, but allow a general discussion led by the children.

◆ Look at prayers from other faiths (see, for example, 'Prayers from the Celtic tradition' on page 50). What sort of things do people pray about, besides giving praise?

◆ Study other aspects of Jewish daily and weekly life which are to do with remembering God, for example the kosher kitchen, the mezuzah (see page 107) and the Sabbath. Note the blessings associated with these. See also the 'Interview with Jeremy Michelson' (page 120).

◆ In a circle, take it in turns to finish the sentence, 'I am thankful that…'.

◆ Discuss some of the themes within the blessings, for example what it is to be wise, and why is it good to have knowledge and learning.

◆ Have an open discussion about why food might be so central to thanksgiving.

◆ Encourage the children to write their own version of a thanksgiving in the same form, directed either to God or to someone who looks after and provides for them. It is better to avoid the use of 'blessed' except in relation to God, but other words could be used, for example: 'Kind are you, Mum, feeder of the family, who buys pizza for tea'; 'Good are you, Jean, minder of many children, who lets us play in the park on the way home.'

Further literacy ideas

◆ Discuss the meaning of words such as 'good', 'loving', 'blessed', 'power' and 'king', noting how their meaning is different, but related, in different contexts. For example, 'Those are a good pair of shoes', 'God is good', 'That is a good child', and 'Good!' as an exclamation. Help the children to make word banks of related words they associate with these words.

◆ Look at the use of the capital letter in association with God in religious texts. When else is the capital letter used?

◆ Discuss the inversion of 'blessed are you' from the form you would expect in everyday use, 'You are blessed'. You might 'play with' other expressions to see what they sound like inverted, for example, 'you are kind' becoming 'kind are you'.

◆ Ask the children to write about the feelings, sights and smells they associate with one of the occasions listed.

Jewish Laws

Some laws concerning the mezuzah

(as found in the Kitzur Shulhan Arukh and selected by Rabbi Hershel Matt, with additions by Stu Copans)

*Genre
instructions
(rules); text
which also
incorporates
two prayers*

1. A mezuzah is affixed to every door in the house. A room used for personal purposes, such as a bathroom or lavatory, needs no mezuzah on the door.

2. The mezuzah is affixed on the right-hand side as one enters.

3. The mezuzah is affixed within the upper third of the doorpost but must be no less than a handbreadth distant from the top.

4. The mezuzah is affixed in the following manner:

a) Roll the parchment from the end of the sentence to the beginning, that is, from the last word – Ehad – towards the first word – Shema – so that the word Shema is on top.

b) Put it in the tube.

c) Fasten it to the doorpost diagonally, having the top line containing the word Shema toward the house and the last word toward the outside. If the doorpost is not wide enough, the mezuzah may be fastened to it perpendicularly. The mezuzah is not considered valid if it is merely suspended. It must be fastened with nails at the top and at the bottom.

5. Before affixing the mezuzah, say the blessing (see below). If several mezuzot are to be affixed at the one time, the saying of one blessing before affixing the first mezuzah will suffice for all. If the mezuzah happens to fall by itself from the doorpost, the blessing must be repeated when it is affixed again.

6. A building not used for a permanent residence needs no mezuzah. Therefore a sukkah made for the holiday of Sukkot requires no mezuzah. It has become the custom today, however, to affix mezuzot to public buildings, i.e. community centres and synagogues.

7. Every mezuzah must be inspected twice every seven years to be sure that the writing is still legible. You must, therefore, make provision for opening the mezuzah to inspect the parchment.

8. In the Diaspora, a mezuzah must be put up within thirty days of moving into a house.

9. In Israel, a mezuzah must be put up immediately on moving into a house.

10. The scroll in the mezuzah should be written on parchment by a scribe.

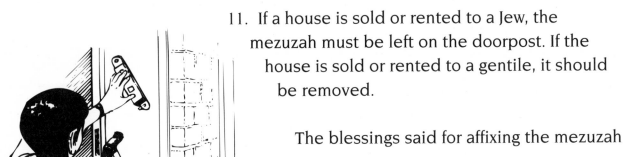

11. If a house is sold or rented to a Jew, the mezuzah must be left on the doorpost. If the house is sold or rented to a gentile, it should be removed.

The blessings said for affixing the mezuzah are:
Blessed are You, Lord our G_d, King of the Universe, who has sanctified us with His commandments, commanding us to affix the mezuzah.

Blessed are You, Lord our G_d, King of the Universe, who has kept us alive and sustained us and permitted us to reach this moment.

12. Some have the custom of touching the mezuzah with their fingers and then bringing their fingers to their lips as they enter and leave. This reminds them of God's omnipresence.

The Jewish Catalog, compiled and edited by Richard Seigel, Michael and Sharon Strassfeld, published by The Jewish Publication Society of America

Jewish Laws

Genre
instructions (rules); text which also incorporates two prayers

RE objectives

◆ To develop awareness of texts about ritual, and to learn to interpret such texts.

◆ To develop understanding of a Jewish ritual.

Previous knowledge

Some knowledge of Judaism: the scriptures, the Law would be useful.

Background notes

You will need a mezuzah or picture of a mezuzah.

This text probably could not be used on its own but it can complement a unit of work on Judaism, or it can build on prior knowledge and be a useful way of revisiting and revising earlier work.

The mezuzah (pl. mezuzot) is the small box containing the words of the Shema nailed to the doorposts in the Jewish home. The Shema is the first of the Ten Commandments, found in Deuteronomy 6:4, so called after the first word in the Hebrew text, shema or 'hear'. The words are written by hand on parchment in Hebrew by an authorized scribe and they read: 'Hear O Israel, The Lord is our God, the Lord alone. You shall love the Lord your God with all your heart and with all your soul and with all your might.' It must contain no mistakes.

There are many mitzvot or commandments. The most important are the 613 to be found in the Torah – the five books of Moses. Other rules are those found in the Talmud, the 4–5th century commentaries on the Torah, and in the subsequent teachings of the rabbis as they sought to interpret the laws and apply them to everyday life. These rules are called halakah. This text is an example of such a set of rules. The initial law to 'write these words upon your doorpost' (Deuteronomy 6: 9) has been translated into ritual rules which can be put into practice.

The Jewish Catalog is a book which is written as a resource for Jews in a way that 'opens options for personal creativity and contemporary utilization of directives' (page 9). It contains guidance, recipes, folklore and rules.

(Note that G_d is written without the vowel, out of respect for many Jews who will not write the full word because it is a name to be honoured.)

Key words

Mezuzah; doorpost; Shema; blessing.

Discussing the text

◆ Show the children a mezuzah (or illustration of one) and ask them to tell you anything they might know about it. Make sure you link it to Judaism in the course of the discussion. You can then introduce the text as one which is about the mezuzah. The title indicates that the editors are not only acknowledging their sources, but also the claim by which these rules are authoritative. Note that the word 'mezuzah' is a Hebrew word with no direct English equivalent. Its plural, mezuzot, reflects its Hebrew form.

◆ Look at the title of the book from which the text is taken. Note the American spelling of 'catalog'. Discuss briefly what is involved in compilation and editing.

◆ Read through the rules together. Words and phrases possibly needing attention might be:

affixed fixed onto

diaspora a term used to describe any people who are not living in their land of origin (for example, one can speak of the Chinese diaspora as the communities of Chinese outside China).

valid something that is right and fit for its purpose

parchment animal skin smoothed and prepared for writing, or high grade paper made to look like parchment.

make provision to allow for

◆ Ask the children about the genre of the text by asking for whom it is written, drawing out that it is written for people who want to put up mezuzot, not as an information text for an outsider. How can we tell?

◆ Re-read the text and ask the children, in turn, for something they have learned about the mezuzah from the text (for example, that it is nailed to doorposts).

◆ Ask them to suggest reasons why Jewish families would fix mezuzot to their doorposts, and for their own reasoning which lies behind their opinion. Which items in their own houses show their commitments, the things they think are important?

Further RE activities

◆ Look at the text again and discuss two of the main interpretations of the significance of the mezuzah:

– it is something which is a sign of God's protection and blessing on the home

– it is a way to be reminded of God's presence and to keep his laws.

◆ Encourage the children to talk and write about their own home. Are there any 'house' rules? How do people show care for one another in the home?

◆ Look at the Shema (Deuteronomy 6:4) and the command to write these words on your doorpost (Deuteronomy 6:9). Ask: 'What is it that is so important that it must be written on doorposts?' Note that these words are the opening of the ten commandments. Ask the children to suggest what it

might signify to love the God with heart and soul and might. (Different translations will give slightly different words.) Then encourage the children to make a small box and to write inside it words they think are very important.

◆ Raise with the children the problem of not knowing quite what rules sometimes mean. How do we know how to obey them? (For example when you are told to keep your work neat – what does that mean?) Tell them how the rabbis (teachers) have sought to help Jews obey this commandment by developing further rules. Look at the tefillin as another example (see 'Interview with Jeremy Michelson', page 120, see also *100 Ideas for RE* and 'Rules' in *REAL Junior Teachers' Handbook*, see the Resources list, page 160).

◆ Give the children a general rule, for example, 'Keep the classroom tidy' and ask them to write out in detail sub-rules for observing it, if possible incorporating a procedure such as that described for fixing the mezuzah. For example, 'replace all books on the shelf' and 'put pens back in tubs'.

◆ Discuss with the children where laws come from. Why do we need them? Who has the authority to make them? In this case it is believed that the original law came directly from God, and other laws came under God's guidance via rabbis.

◆ Look in more detail at the blessings (page 102 and the idea of giving blessing for all aspects of one's life. (See also the Psalm on page 99.)

◆ Discuss the difference between laws and customs. Ask the children to give examples from their own everyday lives.

Further literacy ideas

◆ Look at the words which are transliterated from the Hebrew and are explicitly religious vocabulary.

◆ Look at the word 'residence'. Ask the children to make up list of places which are residences.

◆ Note the use of numbers and letters when writing out rules. Why do people put numbers and letters? Why has the author changed from numbers to letters in number 4?

◆ Look for words which show something is a command. How do we know that number 12 is not a command?

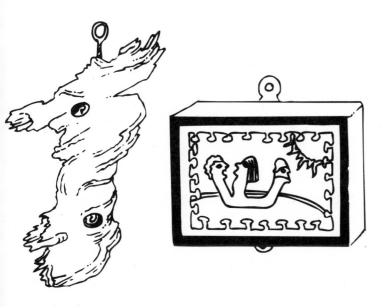

The Dog and the Cat

Genre
fiction;
traditional
tale

Why are the cat and dog enemies? Why do they hiss, spit and growl at each other? It was not always so.

Long, long ago when the world was newly created, dogs and cats maintained a friendly relationship with each other; it was only later on that they became enemies. In the beginning a dog and a cat were partners and they shared with each other whatever they had. It once happened that neither could find anything to eat for three days.

Thereupon the dog suggested that they should dissolve their partnership. The cat should go and live with Adam, in whose house there would surely be enough to eat, while the dog should seek his fortune elsewhere. Before they separated they took an oath never to go to the same master.

The cat took up her abode with Adam, and she found sufficient mice in his house to satisfy her appetite. Seeing how useful she was in driving away the mice, Adam treated her most kindly.

The dog on the other hand, saw bad times. The first night after their separation he spent the night in the cave of a wolf who granted him a night's lodging. At night the dog caught the sound of steps, and he reported it to his host, who told him to get rid of the intruders. They were wild animals. The dog feared he would lose his life, so dismayed he fled from the house of the wolf and tried to take refuge with a monkey, but the monkey wouldn't even grant him one night's lodging. The fugitive was forced to seek the hospitality of a sheep. Again the dog heard steps in the middle of the night. He rose up to chase the intruders who turned out to be wolves. The dog's barking told the wolves where the sheep was, so that the dog innocently caused the death of the sheep.

Now he had lost his last friend. Night after night he begged for shelter, without ever finding a home. Finally he decided to go to the house of Adam, who granted him shelter for one night.

When wild animals approached the house under cover of darkness, the dog began to bark, Adam woke and with his bow and arrow drove them away. Recognizing the dog's usefulness, Adam bade him remain with him always.

But as soon as the cat spied the dog in Adam's house, she began to quarrel with him and reproach him with having broken his oath to her. Adam did his best to pacify the cat. He told her that he himself had invited the dog to make his home there, and assured her that she would be in no way the loser by the dog's presence; he wanted them both to stay with him. But it was impossible to appease the cat. The dog promised not to touch anything that was intended for her. She insisted that they could not live in one and the same house with a thief like the dog. Bickerings between the cat and the dog became the order of the day. Finally the dog could stand it no longer, and he left Adam's house and took himself to Seth's. By Seth he was welcomed kindly and from Seth's house, he continued to make efforts at reconciliation with the cat. In vain. The enmity between the first cat and the first dog has been transmitted to all their descendants until this very day.

Adapted from Louis Ginzberg's Legends of the Bible, Jewish Publication Society

The Dog and the Cat

Genre
*fiction;
traditional
tale*

RE objectives

◆ To develop familiarity and understanding of legends associated with creation.

◆ To consider tension between animals and between people. .

Previous knowledge

None needed; although the text has more interest if the children are familiar with the account of creation in Genesis.

Background notes

There are literally hundreds of legends associated with the Bible, both the Hebrew Bible and the New Testament, many of them two thousand years old or more. This story comes from a collection made at the beginning of the 20th century by Louis Ginzberg who sought to gather 'haggadah' (stories) from all over the Jewish world.

Legends also supplement the authorized texts in conveying teachings and insights within a religion. It is perhaps an essential feature of legends that their original authors are anonymous. The stories in Ginzberg's collection were collected and rewritten by him but he was not their originator. Legends have years of oral tradition behind them.

This particular story, explaining the enmity between dog and cat, is one among many about the creation of the world and its first days, a story which in itself only takes up the first two chapters of Genesis. It is typical of many creation stories in that it offers a reason for a state of affairs in the world today. (Another example of such a story is that of the Garden of Eden, which tells why there is death, and enmity between the snake and man.)

Key words

Enmity.

Discussing the text

◆ Look at the source of the story, noting the religion from which it comes. Ask the children to give their ideas on what a legend is. Draw out that these are not stories found in this form in the Bible or Torah itself but are stories linked to people and events in the Bible. Tell them that the story is hundreds of years old.

◆ Read the story together. Clarify any language that the children may not understand, such as 'abode', 'pacify', 'enmity' and 'transmitted'.

◆ Let the children talk freely about the content of the story.

◆ Discuss what it is about the story that suggests it is a legend, even without knowing where it came from.

◆ Ask the children why they think people made up stories such as this one. What do they think this story is trying to teach?

Further RE activities

◆ Ask the children to look to the Bible and other collections of stories that explain why things are as they are. Discuss the similarities or differences. (For example compare the story of Adam and Eve with creation stories from other religions.)

◆ Why do animals fight with each other and why do humans fight with each other? Look for reasons suggested by the story and ask the children to suggest other reasons.

Further literacy ideas

◆ Note the lack of any direct speech in the telling of the story and discuss why this is. (Perhaps because the writer did not want the reader to think that animals spoke at this time – though the snake does in the garden of Eden in the biblical account – or it could simply be his own style.) Turn some of the indirect speech into direct speech.

◆ Pick out some words from the text, for example 'enmity', 'dissolved' and 'oath', and look for synonyms.

◆ Look at the sympathies of the writer. Does he seem to sympathize with the cat or dog or neither?

◆ Help the children to write a version from the cat's viewpoint or the dog's.

◆ Look at the elements of style which are typical of a legend, notably the beginning and the end, and the personifications of animals.

◆ Read the children another aetiological story (a story which tells how things began) such as one from Kipling's *Just So Stories*. Note that although Kipling's stories are similar in form to Ginzberg's, they are not strictly speaking legends since Kipling made them up himself.

◆ Begin a class collection of stories and jokes that that the children first heard rather than read.

◆ Ask the children to write their own 'just so story'.

Reb Meir Bear

Genre
traditional
tale

A stranger wandered into town leading a huge brown bear. The beast had an iron ring through his nose with a heavy chain attached to it. Every afternoon the stranger led the bear into the market place. Playing upon a flute, he put the animal through his tricks. The bear danced, stood up on his hind legs, waved his forelegs, begged money from passers-by, and performed other antics for the amusement of the townspeople.

It was on a Friday afternoon when the bear, apparently hungry, refused to dance. The stranger beat him mercilessly but the bear did not budge. Among the townspeople who stood by watching was Rabbi Meir, the richest merchant in town, known for his piety, generosity and good deeds.

"Why do you beat this poor, hungry animal?" he asked angrily.

"If you don't like it, you can buy the bear and feed him milk and honey," the stranger sneered.

"How much will you take for him?" asked Reb Meir.

"Twenty gold pieces," the stranger snapped, never thinking that the Jewish merchant would pay that sum.

"I will pay your price," the merchant replied.

Digging into his pocket, Reb Meir counted out twenty gold pieces, took hold of the chain and led the bear to his house.

"I have brought a guest for the Sabbath," Reb Meir told his astonished family, as he brought the bear into the courtyard.

He tied the bear by the chain, went into the house to change his clothes and went off to attend the services at the synagogue. When he returned, he led the bear into the house, recited the Kiddush, washed his hands, pronounced the blessing over the hallah, cut it into pieces and, as was his custom, distributed the pieces to all of the members of the family. The bear, too, was handed a large piece.

Thus it went for the entire Sabbath. The bear ate at Reb Meir's table, was treated like a member of the family, and in the evening, at the end of the Sabbath, the pious merchant led the bear out into the forest, removed the chain and said, "Go in peace, bear, and do no harm to good people."

Time passed and Reb Meir and his partner set out on a journey. For some strange reason, they lost their way in a forest. After wandering aimlessly for more than two days, Reb Meir suggested that since it was Friday night and the Sabbath was near, they should stop to rest. To this the partner would not agree. They decided therefore to divide their food and money. The partner took the wagon and the horse and went off, leaving Reb Meir alone in the forest.

As the sun went down Reb Meir began to recite the Friday evening prayers, welcoming Queen Sabbath. Suddenly a heavy paw descended on his shoulder. He turned and lo and behold! – there was a huge brown bear staring at him with mild, almost human eyes. Reb Meir immediately recognized his Sabbath guest of several years before.

"Good Sabbath," said Reb Meir to the bear.

The bear growled pleasantly, picked up Reb Meir's bags and carried them to a cave which was obviously his home. There, Reb Meir spent the Sabbath as the guest of the bear.

On Saturday night after Reb Meir had recited the Havdalah, the bear again picked up Reb Meir's bags and led him out of the forest. As dawn rose they reached the edge of the woods. A strange sight met Reb Meir's eyes. He saw his partner tied to a tree. Near him a band of robbers was dividing his goods. Before Reb Meir had time to cry out, the bear swept down on the robbers, killing some and frightening away the others. Reb Meir untied his partner and within a few days they reached home safely.

From that day on, Reb Meir was known as Reb Meir Bear, and that name has remained with the family ever since.

By David Einhorn from The Kids' Catalog of Jewish Holidays by David A Adler, published 1996 by The Jewish Publication Society

Reb Meir Bear

Genre
traditional tale

RE objectives

◆ To gain understanding of a Jewish interpretation of key rituals.
◆ To reflect on the importance of treating animals kindly.

Previous knowledge

None strictly necessary, but some knowledge of Shabbat (the Sabbath) would be useful.

It is also worth noting that it is not clear whether this tale is an old one or one created in traditional form.

Key words

Reb; Sabbath; synagogue.

Discussing the text

◆ Look at the title and wonder with the children about it. What can it mean? Is this somebody's name? Is it a story about a bear? Explain that 'Reb' means 'rabbi' or teacher. Check that they know what a merchant is, telling them that the story is about a merchant.

◆ Read the story to the children, with them either listening or following it from the text.

◆ Recap the story with them, perhaps by summarizing briefly each scene and asking them to imagine it.

◆ Ask for their first reactions to the story, comments and questions. Here they may raise the question of whether it is true or not, which might then lead into a discussion about it. From this the genre of a legend or folk tale might emerge (see Introduction, page 7): it is a story about an ordinary person, but there is a supernatural or magical element to it.

◆ Discuss what the author presumes his readers will know already and therefore doesn't explain. Whether or not they raise questions about the Sabbath and its observance will depend on whether they have studied the Sabbath before. At this point link it to Judaism if the children have not raised this already.

◆ Divide most of the children into groups to talk about the different characters in the story, such as the stranger, merchant, wife, children, robber and companion. Ask the remainder of the class to pretend they are reporters and ask them to make up interview questions. Interviewers then interview other children as though they were the characters they discussed.

◆ Help the children to write the story from the perspective of one of the characters or a newspaper report based on the story.

Further RE activities

◆ Discuss with the children what the reader learns about the Sabbath and how it should be kept.

◆ Find out about and discuss:

– the personification of the Sabbath as a queen who should be welcomed to the house. Learn a Sabbath song that welcomes her.

– the two rituals of the Sabbath: sharing hallah bread and the passing round of the spice box at Havdalah. Make both.

◆ Then discuss:

– the rights and wrongs of using animals for entertainment.

– ways that people show kindness to animals.

◆ Focus on other texts. Find the story of St Gerasimus and the lion (sometimes also told of St Jerome, see the Resources list on page 160) and look at the Aesop's fable 'The lion and the mouse' and the key difference between them: in the St Gerasimus story there is a spontaneous act of kindness, in the Aesop fable, the mouse bargains for his life with the lion.

Further literacy ideas

◆ Write a class or individual character profile of the Rabbi, drawing on words and actions found in the text. (He could be described as eccentric as well as kind and pious.)

◆ Discuss some of the specific words that might be unfamiliar to the children, distinguishing between words that are specific to Judaism and its rituals, for example, 'Kiddush' and 'halla', and words in general usage, for example, 'antics', 'mercilessly', 'recited', 'pious' and 'aimlessly'. Look to the context for meaning and then direct the children to the dictionary to check.

◆ Look at the process of turning a noun into an adjective with the addition of the suffix '-less', and then into an adverb though adding '-ly' using the example of 'mercilessly' and 'aimlessly'. Introduce or recall the suffix '-ful' to show the opposite. Encourage the children to 'play' with different words. They should use familiarity with the language and/or dictionaries to check whether they are real words or not (for example, 'homeless' is a real word, 'homeful' is not; 'hope' can take either suffix).

◆ Identify words in the text, including verbs, that suggest feelings and attitudes, for example 'astonished', 'sneered', 'snapped', 'emotions'. Ask the children to suggest other words to express the feelings and attitudes of the Rabbi's children, the second merchant and so on.

◆ Look at time phrases in the text, from the specific 'It was on a Friday afternoon' to the more general 'time passed'. Draw out the way narratives often have to indicate time frames.

◆ Discuss the idea of setting the scene in a narrative. How does this writer do it? What do we learn about from the start?

Interview with Jeremy Michelson –

Education Officer, Jewish Museum, Manchester

Genre
non-fiction;
personal
viewpoint

I wear the kippah as a constant reminder of G_d. Strictly speaking you only have to wear it when saying prayers and blessings but since I never know when I am going to need to say a blessing, I wear it all day. For example I say a blessing whenever I [ritually] wash my hands and I never know when I will need to wash my hands.

The kippah is a permanent reminder to myself of who I am and what I am. It keeps me on the straight and narrow so that I always behave properly and bring honour to G_d.

I wear it too as a reminder of G_d's eternal presence. G_d is higher than us. We human beings think we run the show but we don't – G_d does.

I say blessings for several reasons. Sometimes it is a way of asking G_d's permission to use something. For example, we ask G_d's permission to eat food by saying a blessing and at the end of the Sabbath we say a blessing to ask G_d's permission to light a fire again. Saying blessings can also be a way of thanking G_d for giving us the commandments to fulfil. We Jews believe that having the commandments is a special responsibility, a calling which makes demands of us but also brings its own rewards.

Saying blessings makes me rejoice in G_d's creativity. The world is a wonderful place and we are often too busy to enjoy it. When I say a blessing I have to stop to appreciate it. Blessings help me focus on the idea that everything is part of a bigger scheme, even if I don't always understand it. For example I find it difficult to understand the purpose of slugs, but I believe that they are part of G_d's creation.

There are three elements to the tefillin. I bind G_d's words near my brain, near my heart and onto my hands. It reminds me to harness my intellect, my emotions and my actions to the will of G_d. All three things are subordinated to G_d's will. One of our ancient rabbis, Rabbi Gamiel, said long ago 'Do G_d's will as if it were your will, so that he may do your will as if it were his will'.

We don't wear the tefillin on the Sabbath in the synagogue because of the practical problem of carrying them. We are not allowed to carry things outside the home on the Sabbath, and the tefillin are too expensive to have one at home and one at the synagogue.

Whereas we do wear the tallit on the Sabbath. Firstly, lots of people keep one at the synagogue itself. Secondly, it is possible to wear the tallit on the street, rather than carry it. Wearing the tallit with all its tassels is another reminder to keep G_d's laws.

All these rituals are a form of discipline. Of course sometimes it is possible to observe them just out of habit, to pray and say the blessings without concentrating. However, generally it is a form of training so that it influences every aspect of life.

And of course there is a lot of joy in observing the rituals. The festivals are really something to look forward to. Hardly a month goes by without one festival or other, and I would really miss having the Sabbath. It is a time to really enjoy being with the family, a meal to linger over, not to rush like the rest of the week. It is also time to take it easy, a time of spiritual rejuvenation, a time to sit and read the Torah.

Glossary

Kippah (yarmulke) head covering worn by Jewish men

Tefillin small leather boxes containing a scroll with the Shema written on it, which Jewish men bind to their forehead and left arm when they pray

Tallit prayer shawl with knotted fringes worn by Jewish men when they pray

Shema the first commandment, found in the Bible, Deuteronomy 6:8–9

Sabbath the Jewish day of rest and worship; the seventh day of the week (Saturday)

Interview with Jeremy Michelson

Genre
non-fiction;
personal
viewpoint

RE objective

◆ To gain understanding of a Jewish interpretation of key rituals.

Previous knowledge

Children will need to have been introduced to the tefillin and tallit, and to the blessings (page 102).

Background notes

Judaism has many ritual practices which are part and parcel of its daily life. The majority have their roots in the Torah, the holy book. The tefillin are worn in response to the injunction in Deuteronomy 6:8–9 to bind the words of Deuteronomy 6:4 to the head, the heart and to the hand. These words are called Shema. The tallit, a fringed prayer shawl, is worn in response to Numbers 15:38–39. Blessings are said throughout the day.

Even where a ritual is widely observed, its meaning to any individual observer is personal, though informed by teaching in the synagogue and by studies of the Torah – the Jewish Law – and Rabbinic commentaries on it. Study of the Torah and the rabbis (teachers) has a central place in Jewish spirituality. Thus in this text we have Jeremy Michelson's personal account formed from his experience and influenced by his studies.

The vowel has been omitted in G_d out of deference to Jewish practice.

Key words

Tefillin; Sabbath; blessings; discipline; tallit; ritual.

Discussing the text

◆ Introduce the text as a report of an interview. Perhaps comment on the fact that it is written in the first person, with 'I', but the writer might not be the speaker. What religion does the speaker belong to?

◆ Comment on and explain the absence of the vowel in 'God'.

◆ Read through the text once. It is probably best at this stage not to focus on words the children don't understand, but to get the feel of the text as a whole.

◆ List with the children the items that Jeremy talks about. What do the children know about these items already? (You might have pictures to hand in preparation for this.)

◆ Go back to the difficult words, such as 'subordinated' and 'rejuvenation'. Ask the children to suggest meanings from the context, then to look them up in a dictionary.

◆ Look at the metaphor of harness. Ask the children what it means to harness a horse. What then might it mean to harness your will to somebody else's will?

◆ Ask the children to express in their own words the significance of each item to Jeremy, for example 'Why does he wear the kippah?' 'Why does he say the blessings?'

◆ Children write what they have learned from the interview.

Further RE activities

◆ Remind the children that the words of the Shema are written inside the tefillin. Look up the Shema in Deuteronomy 6:4 and discuss what it might mean.

◆ Read (or re-read) the story of the giving of the Law to Moses in the desert (Exodus 19:16–20:21) and link it with the ideas in the text about discipline and doing God's will. There are several children's versions of the story available, including one in *A Tapestry of Tales* (see the Resources list, page 160).

◆ Ask the children to make their own scroll with important words on it. Let them decide for themselves what are 'important words'.

◆ Look at texts on Mezuzah (for example on page 107), pointing out that both mezuzah and tefillin contain the words of Shema.

◆ Discuss the idea of doing God's will. How does Jeremy think God's will is known? (You will need to go back to the text.) How do the children think that God's will is known? (This might lead on to the idea that different religions have different ideas of what God's will is.)

◆ How can we tell that Jeremy Michelson's religion is very important to him? Encourage the children to discuss the importance that religion has in some people's lives.

◆ Discuss how the children remember things, rules and people. What physical things do they use to remind themselves? What do they want to remember?

◆ Look up the word 'ritual' and discuss it. Help the children to identify their own rituals and reflect on them. What sort of rituals are built into the school day, for example in clothing, in assembly, in the way the day is finished? Set it up so that the children interview each other about a ritual in their home or about something which is important to them (for example, a festival, meal times or evenings).

◆ Discuss the idea of discipline (the word derives from the Latin *discere*, to learn). You might draw the parallel between keeping the Jewish Law, and the Muslim observance of Ramadan, learning self-restraint through fasting.

Further literacy ideas

◆ Draw the children's attention to the words 'permanent' and 'eternal' in paragraphs 2 and 3. Ask them to suggest antonyms to these words. List other words to do with measuring time or indicating length of time.

◆ Taking the example of 'harness my intellect… to the will of G_d', think of other metaphors for linking and cooperating, for example 'all pull together' and 'chain of command'.

◆ Ask the children to suggest the questions the interviewer asked.

◆ Encourage them to rewrite the text in a question and answer format.

slam

Islam began with a text and is based on a text: the Qur'an, which is held to have been written by God and revealed to the Prophet Muhammad from the time of his first vision at the age of forty, around AD610, and throughout the rest of his life. As the words are regarded as those of God himself, the Qur'an is read and studied in the original Arabic and translations are never used in worship. The poetic style and beauty of the language are regarded as indications of its divine origin. The Qur'an give guidance about everyday life, as well as stories and prayers. Muslim rituals are rooted in the Qur'an, as seen in the text on fasting and the practice of Hajj. The text taken from the editorial of an Islamic magazine for children illustrates the centrality of the Qur'an and the value given to the Arabic language.

Muslim children begin to study Arabic and the Qur'an in Mosque schools from quite an early age, and learn to say prayers from the Qur'an in Arabic by joining in the five daily prayer times with their families.

The other main source of Islamic tradition and authority is the collection known as the Hadith: carefully checked traditions about the words and actions (sunna) of the Prophet Muhammad. Wherever the Qur'an gives no specific guidance, the Hadith are the next most authoritative source.

British Muslims have made considerable effort to supplement this teaching with accessible material in English for children, and one can buy books of Islamic stories told for children as well as instructional texts, magazines and activity books. We have included selections from an instructional book for Muslim children, and a magazine.

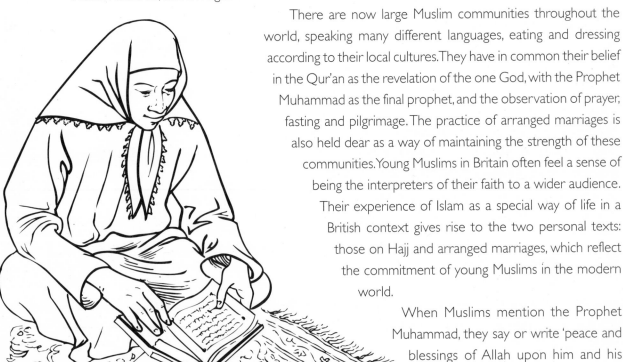

There are now large Muslim communities throughout the world, speaking many different languages, eating and dressing according to their local cultures. They have in common their belief in the Qur'an as the revelation of the one God, with the Prophet Muhammad as the final prophet, and the observation of prayer, fasting and pilgrimage. The practice of arranged marriages is also held dear as a way of maintaining the strength of these communities. Young Muslims in Britain often feel a sense of being the interpreters of their faith to a wider audience. Their experience of Islam as a special way of life in a British context gives rise to the two personal texts: those on Hajj and arranged marriages, which reflect the commitment of young Muslims in the modern world.

When Muslims mention the Prophet Muhammad, they say or write 'peace and blessings of Allah upon him and his family' after his name as a sign of respect.

Qur'an

A translation of a quotation from the Qur'an about fasting

Surah 2 (Baqara, the Cow): 183–85

Genre
*non-fiction;
rules/
commandments*

O you who believe, fasting is prescribed to you as it was prescribed to those before you, so that you may learn self-restraint. Fast for a fixed number of days, but if any of you is ill or on a journey the prescribed number should be made up later. For those whose difficulties prevent them from fasting, the feeding of a poor person is a ransom. He that does good of his own account shall be rewarded, but is better for you to fast if only you knew it.

Ramadan is the month in which the Qur'an was sent down as a guide to mankind, also clear signs for guidance and to judge between right and wrong. So every one of you who is present (at his home) during that month should spend it fasting but if anyone is ill or on a journey the prescribed period should be made up by days later. Allah intends every facility for you. He does not want to put you to difficulties. He wants you to complete the prescribed period and to glorify Him in that He has guided you.

Qur'an

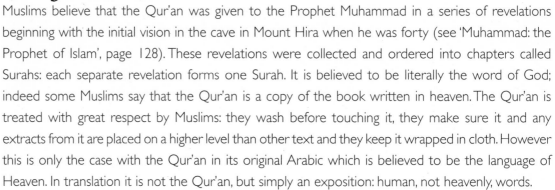

RE objectives

◆ To know the Qur'an is a sacred book which gives guidance to Muslims.
◆ To understand the importance of fasting during Ramadan.

Previous knowledge

An introduction to Ramadan and the month of fasting would be useful.

Background notes

Muslims believe that the Qur'an was given to the Prophet Muhammad in a series of revelations beginning with the initial vision in the cave in Mount Hira when he was forty (see 'Muhammad: the Prophet of Islam', page 128). These revelations were collected and ordered into chapters called Surahs: each separate revelation forms one Surah. It is believed to be literally the word of God; indeed some Muslims say that the Qur'an is a copy of the book written in heaven. The Qur'an is treated with great respect by Muslims: they wash before touching it, they make sure it and any extracts from it are placed on a higher level than other text and they keep it wrapped in cloth. However this is only the case with the Qur'an in its original Arabic which is believed to be the language of Heaven. In translation it is not the Qur'an, but simply an exposition: human, not heavenly, words.

You will need a copy of the Qur'an (this is optional but helpful).

Key words

Qur'an; fasting; guidance; prescribed; Ramadan.

Discussing the text

◆ Show the children a Qur'an, remembering to treat it with respect. Ask the children what they recall about it, then introduce the text (without showing it yet) as one that comes from the Qur'an. What language should it be in? (See notes above.)
◆ Look at the title of the text – why does it mention 'translation'?
◆ Look at the word 'Surah' (chapter) and the verse reference. Perhaps briefly discuss why the book is divided into chapters and verses, drawing out that this is a way of finding references in it more easily. Each Surah has a name based on the first word, but the numbers make it easier to find and refer to.
◆ Look at the opening sentence. Who is this passage addressed to? Discuss the meaning of the word 'prescribed' – perhaps building on the children's knowledge of the word 'prescription'.
◆ Read the first paragraph. What can be learned from it about the fasting? List the items. Explore the meaning of the word 'ransom' in the context. Does it mean paying to return a kidnap victim? If not, what does it mean?
◆ Look at the opening sentence of the second verse. What do we learn about the purpose of the Qur'an from it? Read though the rest of the paragraph which reiterates what has been said before.

Look at the meaning of the word 'facility' putting it in the context of 'Allah does not want to put you in difficulties'.

◆ Let the children suggest why Muslims value Ramadan, taking ideas both from the text and from other knowledge.

◆ Ask the children what they have learned from studying the text that they didn't know before. Encourage them to think of specific information from the text, but also emphasize to them that the primary reason for observing Ramadan is to obey the Qur'an.

Further RE activities

◆ Ask a Muslim child in the class to talk about their experience of Ramadan. If there are no Muslim children in the school, invite in a Muslim speaker, visit a mosque or establish an e-mail link with Muslim children in another school. Help them plan the interview questions.

◆ Revisit the story of the first revelation to the Prophet Muhammad, known as the Night of Power. This can be found in *A Tapestry of Tales* (see the Resources list, page 160).

◆ Discuss the idea of books of guidance. Why do Muslims believe that the Qur'an is the best book of guidance? What books do the children have that contain rules or guidance? Which ones are important to them? (For example a manual relating to some hobby or interest, such as how to take care of a pet.) Draw out that the guidance in this passage is about how to live.

◆ Ask the children to make a small book filled with rules they feel are important in life.

◆ Discuss ideas of self-discipline. Why do the children think Muslims prefer to fast together, so that often they will fast even when they are not feeling well, despite the exemption?

◆ In Ramadan, Muslims are also encouraged to think about the poor and needy. Who do the children think are needy in our world? How can the children help them?

Further literacy ideas

◆ Look at words to do with rules and commandments.

◆ Ask the children to find other words with the prefix 'pre-'.

◆ Look at other words based on 'script/scribe', for example 'scripture', 'scribe', 'scribble' and 'script'.

◆ Look at ways of addressing the presumed audience in a text, such as 'dear' and 'to', and the use of the second person, 'you', characteristic of prescriptive texts.

◆ Look at how books are laid out for referencing. Discuss why books such as the Bible and the Qur'an have been given chapters and verses rather than page numbers. (Because of the need for a common reference system despite many editions and translations into many languages. Note that versification of the Bible was a late addition and not in the original text.) Conversely, in Sikhism, the Guru Granth Sahib is referred to by page number, and every copy is written with the same pagination.

Genre
non-fiction;
information
biography

Muhammad: the Prophet of Islam

AD570–632

The Prophet Muhammad was born to the Quraysh tribe in what is now Saudi Arabia in the second half of the 6th century. Orphaned when young, he was raised by an uncle. At the age of twenty he married an older widow, Khadijah, and he gained a reputation as an honest and upright trader whose judgement was respected. At the age of forty, in 610, he told his wife that while praying in a cave at Hira the angel Gabriel (Jibra'il in Arabic) had come to him in a vision. The angel had instructed him to memorize and recite words given to him; words which called people to worship one true God.

Muhammad began to teach this message of the oneness of God in the city of Mecca which, at that time, practised a polytheistic religion. Many people listened to his preaching and followed the new religion. They called themselves Muslims, which means those who obey God. However many others in Mecca opposed Muhammad's teaching and persecuted him. In 622 he and his followers left Mecca and found refuge in the city of Medina. Muslim dates are all calculated from this journey (the Hijrah) in AD622, which is year 1AH (After Hijrah).

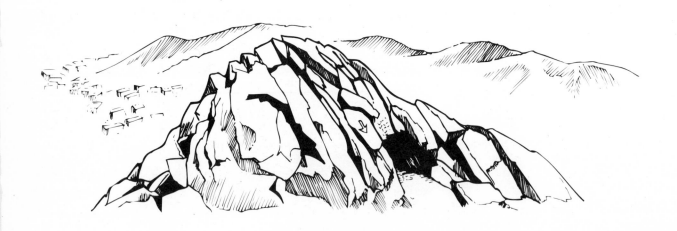

During the next ten years Muhammad was a
preacher, a teacher and a political and military leader. By
AD630 the Muslims had captured Mecca itself and much
of the rest of the area. Muhammad died in 632, having
established Mecca as a Muslim city.

Throughout his life Muhammad continued to teach
his followers words which he believed the Angel Jibra'il
had given to him. He told his followers that there were
times when he felt as though the angel had taken hold
of him, and whispered the words in his ear so that they
became a part of him. It was these words he taught to
his followers. The words were always in a beautiful
Arabic and sounded very different from his ordinary,
everyday speech. Muslims believe that this is a sign that
they came from God himself. The words were written
down and they became the Qur'an.

Muslims believe that Muhammad was God's final
prophet. They do not recognize the claim to
prophethood of anyone after Muhammad, and they
believe that the Qur'an corrects mistakes people made
about earlier prophets such as Jesus. (The Qur'an
teaches that Jesus was a prophet but not the son of
God). To show their respect for Muhammad, Muslims
say 'Peace be upon him' after they say his name. They
do not allow pictures of him, because a picture might
become an object of worship and they believe that only
God should be worshipped.

Many of Muhammad's sayings and teachings, which
do not form part of the Qur'an, were written down and
collected. These are known as the Hadith.

Muhammad: the Prophet of Islam

RE objectives

◆ To encounter the Prophet Muhammad as a historical figure.

◆ To know the special significance of Muhammad in Islam.

Previous knowledge

None is necessary, however, you could use the text in a lesson that follows on from a visit to a mosque or a video clip. The Prophet Muhammad will have been introduced as a significant figure in Islam. Now you are seeking, as a class, to find out more about him.

Background notes

The Prophet Muhammad was an historical figure about whom Muslims make statements of faith. Non-Muslims can accept the facts of his life, such as his marriage to Khadijah, without sharing the belief that he is God's final prophet, or even that God gave a revelation to the Prophet Muhammad.

This text is deliberately written in an informative rather than narrative style.

The dating system BC/AD has been retained since it is the one most commonly used. Some recent books use CE (Christian or common era) and BCE (before common era).

Key words

Qur'an; the Prophet Muhammad; polytheistic; prophet.

Discussing the text

The strategies suggested below are in line with the use of an encyclopaedia as a source for finding answers to questions.

Strategy One: Begin by writing on the board 'the Prophet Muhammad…?'

◆ Pool any class knowledge about the Prophet Muhammad and ask the children to suggest questions which could lead to further knowledge and understanding about him. These questions could range from plain ones of fact: 'Where was he born?' to more subjective ones. Of course, not all the questions will have their answer in the text.

◆ Introduce the text as one in the style of an encyclopaedia.

◆ Read though the text once to the children. Then ask them to read and listen carefully, putting up their hand immediately if they think they hear the answer to any of the questions raised.

◆ At the end of the first reading, look at the questions which have not been answered. Ask the children to list other information found in the text.

Strategy Two (alternative): Introduce the text as biography and discuss the meaning of the term.

◆ Read the text to the class. Ask children to come out and point out where the text tells us that:

The Prophet Muhammad was born in Saudi Arabia.

He had a reputation as an honest trader.

He saw a vision.

He had to leave the city of Mecca.

He became a military leader.

◆ Discuss the meaning of some of the terms in the text, looking first to see if a meaning can be derived from the context. Note that 'vision' and 'prophet' have different meanings in a religious context and an ordinary one. You might ask the children the difference between a prime minister having a vision for his country, and the vision in this text. In the same way, 'prophet' can mean someone who sees into the future but does not necessarily mean this. Its primary religious meaning is 'someone who speaks words from God'.

◆ Other words and phrases which may need discussion are: 'vision', 'polytheistic', 'prophet', 'preacher', 'political' and 'military leader'.

◆ Look more closely at the paragraph beginning 'throughout his life Muhammad continued to teach…'. Ask the children for the meaning they made of the text.

◆ Point out that the text reveals some facts about the Prophet Muhammad's life but also tells us what Muslims believe about the Prophet Muhammad. List some of the things which Muslims believe about the Prophet Muhammad and discuss them.

◆ Discuss whether the text is written by a Muslim or a non-Muslim and for which audience.

◆ Ask the children to identify four key words which would aid retrieval of the text were it on a CD-Rom or the Internet.

Further RE activities

◆ Make a timeline of the Prophet Muhammad's life.

◆ Investigate prophets in the Muslim and Biblical tradition, such as Abraham, Noah and Moses.

◆ Listen to a call to prayer in Arabic. Look at examples of Arabic calligraphy – it is an art form in its own right. Find out about children going to school to learn to read the Qur'an.

◆ Read some children's versions of Hadith, such as 'Muhammad Washing' and 'The Thirsty Camel' in *A Tapestry of Tales* (see the Resources list, page 160).

◆ Find out more about Saudi Arabia and its significance for Muslims today, especially the towns of Mecca and Medina.

◆ Encourage the children to use encyclopaedias to find information about other religious leaders, for example, Jesus and Guru Nanak.

◆ Discuss the fact that the Prophet Muhammad wanted to share his beliefs with others. Ask the children if there is something they think is so important that they would like everyone to agree with them. (An example might be, 'Everyone should be kind to animals' – but allow the children a chance to make their suggestions first.)

◆ Look at the text and discuss where a Christian would agree with a Muslim about the Prophet Muhammad and where they might disagree. Encourage the children to acknowledge and discuss the fact that different religions have different beliefs.

Further literacy ideas

◆ Look at polytheism (many gods) and monotheism (one god). Suggest the children use dictionaries to find other words beginning with the prefixes 'poly-' and 'mono-'.

◆ Point out that the spelling of 'Mecca' in the text is not the only version of the name that is current today. 'Makkah' is often preferred by Muslims – it depends on how one transliterates the Arabic name. Look at idea of anglicizing foreign words, including the names of cities, for example Vienna/Wien.

◆ Compare the style of the text with an account of the Prophet Muhammad's life written in a more narrative style (see *A Tapestry of Tales*, the Resources list, page 160).

Wuḍū

Published by the Muslim Educational Trust

Genre
*non-fiction
procedural
text;
instruction*

Before we can begin to say *Salah*, we must first prepare ourselves. This preparation includes making sure we are clean, and this is done by carrying out *Wuḍū*.

Wuḍū (ablution) is essential for performing *Salah*; we cannot offer our *Salah* without first making *Wuḍū*. These are the steps to take:

a. Make *Niyyah* (intention) saying 'Bismillahir rahmanir rahim' (In the name of Allah, the most Merciful, the most Kind); then wash both hands up to the wrists three times making sure that water has reached between the fingers.

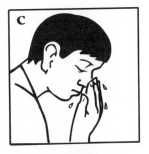

b. Put a handful of water into the mouth and rinse it thoroughly three times.

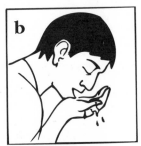

c. Sniff water into the nostrils three times to clean them and then wash the tip of the nose three times.

d. Wash the face three times from right ear to left ear and from forehead to throat.

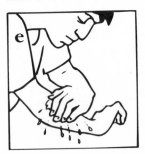

e. Wash the right arm, and then the left arm, thoroughly from wrist to elbow three times.

f. Move the palm of the wet hand over the head, starting from the top of the forehead to the back and pass both hands over the back of the head to the neck.

g. Rub wet fingers into the grooves of both ears and holes and also pass the wet thumbs behind the ears.

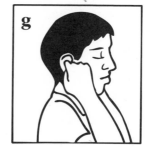

h. Pass the backs of the wet hands over the nape.

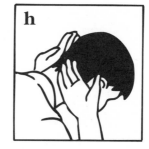

i. Wash both feet to the ankles, starting from the right and making sure that water has reached between the toes and all other parts of the feet.

If you did a complete *Wuḍū* before putting on your socks, it is not necessary to take them off every time you repeat *Wuḍū*. It is enough to wipe the upper part of the socks with wet hands. Such *Wuḍū* lasts for twenty four hours only (three days if on a journey) but a fresh *Wuḍū* must be made after the socks are taken off.

At the end of the *Wuḍū* recite:

"Ash hadu an la ilaha lahu wahdahu la sharikalahu wa ash hadu anna muhammadan 'abduhu wa rasuluhu." (I bear witness that there is no god but Allah and He is the one and has no partner and I bear witness that Muhammad is His servant and messenger.)

Wuḍū

Genre
non-fiction procedural text; instruction

RE objective

◆ To develop knowledge of prayer rituals.

Previous knowledge

Some knowledge of Islam and the five daily prayers would be useful.

Background notes

Prayer, or salah, is the second of the five pillars of Islam. Observation of the five set times for formal prayer is seen as a key spiritual duty bringing one closer to God. The time for prayer is determined by the position of the sun. Personal, private prayer at other times of the day, for example giving thanks and seeking guidance, is also encouraged.

Wudu, washing before prayer, is a transition time during which the person moves from a state of concern for the ordinary world, to being physically and mentally ready to pray.

The alphabet used to write English is Roman; it has been used widely in Western Europe from Roman colonization. You may want to refer to it as the Roman alphabet or keep it simple and stick to English.

Key words

Preparation; thoroughly; bear witness; prayer; wudu.

Discussing the text

◆ Look at what can be learned about the subject matter of the text from the pictures and from the title.

◆ Draw the children's attention to the presence of Arabic words, both in the original script (see the very end of the extract) and those that have been transliterated (that is, a foreign word written with English (Roman) letters. Some of the transliterations use extra marks on the letters. These are to help someone pronounce the Arabic correctly, but they can be ignored. Arabic words are also translated into English in parentheses. Explain that the word 'ablution' is an English word not often used in everyday language, but given a special meaning here.

◆ Read through the text with the children, perhaps miming the instructions as you do so.

◆ Focus on the beginning and end of the instructions, noting that the ablutions are carried out in the name of Allah. (Note: Allah is a transliteration of the Arabic word for God.)

◆ Consider the audience for whom the text is written. How can we tell that it is written to instruct Muslims in how to wash before prayer, rather than to inform non-Muslims about how Muslims wash before prayer? You could also discuss with the children the fact that such instruction texts are written for people who don't know what to do already. This text would be used in the education of Muslim children in the correct procedures for prayer and for people who have just become Muslims.

Further RE activities

◆ Ask the children to investigate Muslim prayer further, for example to find the story of the Prophet Muhammad's night vision which is told to explain why Muslims have to pray five times daily, or to find why prayer beads are used.

◆ Look at the posture and actions in prayer, with particular reference to the movements in Muslim prayer. Does it make a difference to how one feels?

◆ Discuss with the children the times people wash and bath, for example before a meal, before touching something precious, at the end of the day to wash away the dirt of the day, at the beginning of the day to start fresh and clean. How do the children feel after a thorough wash? Why do they think many people, not only Muslims, want to wash before they pray?

Further literacy ideas

◆ Look at the features of the layout: paragraphs are given ordered letters suggesting that the order is important and letters link illustrations with an instruction.

◆ Look at the use of verbs in the imperative form ('make', 'put', 'sniff' and so on) which always comes at the beginning of a sentence or phrase. Point out that this form is likely to be found in any set of instructions. Pick out imperative verbs and look at their form.

◆ Look at the way the author has divided the paragraphs in his instructions: each new paragraph indicates a new area of the body.

◆ List other examples of instructional texts. Discuss things for which the children once needed instructions but can now do without instructions.

◆ Ask the children to write instructions for a routine which is automatic for them to tell a visitor to the school or home (or perhaps a visitor from Mars) what to do. For example how to ride a bicycle, how to set a table, how to programme the video, how to set up a game on the computer, or how to choose and borrow a book from the library.

◆ Talk about the difference in feel and tone between texts which command bluntly and those which use softening, modifying words such as 'please' or a different syntax to command, such as 'you may wish to'. Make a collection of instructional texts from several contexts, for example operating instructions, safety rules or rules of games, and look at the similarities and differences.

◆ Look at the conventions used for printing foreign words in italics and their translation in parenthesis. Point out that the last three paragraphs of the extract give first the Arabic in Arabic script, then a transliteration, then a translation.

◆ Look for other examples of words transliterated into English, such as place names and words from other faiths which use a different writing system, for example, Hebrew (Judaism), Sanskrit (Hinduism), and Gurmukhi (Sikhism). Point out that this can account for variations in spelling.

Editorial Al Huroof

Genre
non-fiction:
editorial

Editorial

In The Name of Allah The Beneficent The Most Merciful

All praise is due to Allah and peace be upon the Final Messenger, Muhammad (Sallallahu'alaihi wa sallam), his family, his companions and all those who follow his Way until the Last Day.

After That:

Assalamu 'alaikum

Welcome all Young Seekers of Knowledge to 'Al Huroof', which means 'The Letters', the first Islamic magazine to be launched in the UK for our English speaking Muslim boys and girls between the ages of 6–12 years old.

Packed with a variety of informative, creative & youthful topics to entertain our readers, Al Huroof aims to teach all our young seekers of knowledge the true beauty & wisdom of al-Islam, in a way that is fun for both you and us, insha'Allah.

Al Huroof is dedicated to presenting the correct knowledge of al-Islam, therefore, great care has been taken to use the correct meaning from the Noble Qur'an and the true Ahadith (sayings, actions and approvals) of the Prophet (Sallallahu'alaihi wa sallam). We will be using Islamic words that may be new to some readers, so remember to ask your parents or family to explain anything that you do not understand.

You may also notice that we have kept away from using faces of people and animals or using rude jokes. This is to make sure that we teach and you learn in a way that is blessed and pure.

We pray to Allah, The most High, to help us in our humble efforts. Ameen

ع ظ ط ض ص ش س ز ذ د خ ح ج ث ت ب ا

Glossary

sallallahu'alaihi wa sallam peace and blessings of Allah be upon him

Assalamu 'alaikum Greetings (literally 'peace be with you')

insha'Allah in the name of Allah

Editorial Al Huroof

RE objectives

◆ To appreciate the importance of children learning about the faith in which they are being brought up.

◆ To appreciate that belief is expressed in a choice of words and pictures.

Background notes

Al Huroof is a magazine for young Muslims in Britain. This first edition included sayings of the Prophet, children's stories, games and instructions on how to make a telephone out of string.

   As the first editorial of the magazine, it sets out its editorial stance and policy, as well as hopes for the new reader.

Key words

Allah; Qur'an; knowledge; Islam; Islamic.

Discussing the text

◆ Explain that you are looking at the editorial of a magazine. Talk about what an editorial is – that it is the personal views of the editor. Discuss with the children the role of an editor.

◆ Let them look at the page and glean what they can from it. They will no doubt notice that there are two languages on the page, and that it is something to do with Islam.

◆ Explain the meaning of the Muslim words where it seems appropriate. If the children have heard the words 'peace and blessings of Allah be upon him' they may be able to guess that this is the meaning of words in brackets after 'Muhammad'. Note that Allah is the Arabic word for God but that many Muslims prefer to use it even when speaking English.

◆ Point out the parts which are quotations and those which are the editor's own writing.

◆ Who does the editor hope will read this magazine?

◆ What are the aims of the magazine?

◆ Whose help and guidance does the editor seek in preparing the magazine?

◆ What do you think the editor believes about the Prophet Muhammad and about Allah?

◆ What advice does the editor give to readers if they don't understand an Islamic word?

◆ Why will there be no faces of people and animals in the magazine? (There is a general prohibition in Islam on depicting people especially their faces.)

Further RE activities

◆ Find out more about the Qur'an and the Prophet Muhammad, including why Muslims call him the Final Messenger.

◆ Discuss religious art and symbolism. Identify religions which allow depiction of the human form, for example, Christianity and Hinduism, and those which forbid it especially in places of worship. Look at examples of books by Muslims and see how they have illustrated the book instead.

◆ Discuss the Islamic idea of everything being undertaken in the name of Allah, and learn the phrase insha'Allah.

Further literacy ideas

◆ Draw the children's attention to the features of the layout, asking why they have been used. Talk about the different sizes of print, the different lettering, and the use of Arabic.

◆ Distinguish between Arabic writing and Arabic words written with an English (Roman) alphabet. Note that neither 'Qur'an' nor 'Muhammad' has a standardized spelling in English. Draw attention to 'Ameen', an Arabic word which means 'Amen'.

◆ Make a glossary of some Islamic words, for example 'Qur'an', 'mosque' and 'the Prophet Muhammad'.

◆ Look at the choice of vocabulary used to describe the magazine: 'informative', 'creative' and 'youthful'. What is the editor trying to convey? What words would the children use to describe their favourite magazine?

◆ Look at the features of an editorial, especially in the first issue of a magazine. (It sets out aims of the magazine and its editorial policy.)

◆ Ask the children to imagine a new magazine on a favourite topic and to write and design an editorial page for the first edition.

Going on Hajj

Genre
non-fiction;
autobiographical
information

I went on Hajj with lots of members of my family – aunts, uncles, cousins, my grandparents and my husband. I am twenty and I was especially excited as it was my first time going on Hajj. Some of the others had been before.

We flew from Manchester Airport to Saudi Arabia in a plane filled with pilgrims. Some of the men showed that their pilgrimage had already begun by dressing in the simple white cloth that all male Muslims wear during the Hajj.

Our family though, began our visit in Medina, the birthplace of the Prophet (p.b.u.h). I will never forget the sight of the great mosque in Medina glowing in the dark. Nor will I forget hearing the call to prayer ring out over the city. I have grown up in Manchester and lived there all my life and I have never been anywhere before where the muezzin call out from the top of the minaret.

And it was astonishing, what happened when the call to prayer came. Everyone, everyone stopped what they were doing and rushed to the mosque to prayer. I prayed thanking God for bringing me here and I guess many others were praying in the same way.

Medina was so clean; all the time there was someone sweeping and cleaning the white marble, and there were people everywhere, from all over the world, speaking many different languages. I talked to lots of people who couldn't speak English. I couldn't speak their language, yet somehow we still talked to each other, and learned about each other. It felt like one big family.

After three days in Medina to get used to the climate, we went to Mecca and it was there that our pilgrimage began properly. From that point all the women were dressed simply, our hair and body fully covered, and all the men wore ihram, the white cloth. We were all equal – you couldn't tell who was a peasant

labourer from the countryside in Pakistan, and who was a doctor. You couldn't tell the highly paid businessman from an office cleaner.

And there was no hierarchy, no status – all normal social distinctions ceased in Mecca, while we were on pilgrimage. The boss and his employee were equal. There was no father, no son; a husband was the same as a stranger, except that no one was really a stranger; we were all Muslims together.

They say that the first time you look at the Kaaba in Mecca, anything you ask for will come true.

My grandmother told me:

"Say to God, 'I have come as a guest to your house, whatever I ask for, give it to me.'"

So I had to think carefully about first prayer, although many people say to God, "Whatever I ask for in the future, give me."

It was quite scary at the Kaaba, because it was so crowded – but it was very orderly, everyone walked round the Kaaba in orderly rows. People like to touch the black stone and kiss it. We believe it was a stone that Adam brought from Paradise. I would have liked to touch the stone but I couldn't, there were just too many people. Perhaps I will on my next Hajj.

But that was only the beginning of the Hajj. We did many other things, including going out into the desert and staying in huge tents. It was peaceful and still out there, despite the huge numbers. Everyone spent the time quietly thinking and praying.

So many things, too many to write down here. I came back from Hajj much more committed to God and to my faith. I made a promise that I would show my commitment by wearing a head covering. I have done this ever since.

Adapted from Mariam Bassa

Going on Hajj

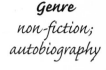
TEACHERS' NOTES

Genre
non-fiction;
autobiography

RE objective
◆ To develop understanding of Hajj.

Previous knowledge
Some knowledge of the Hajj would be useful.

Background notes
This text would either complement a unit of work in RE on the Hajj or it could be used to revisit and revise earlier teaching.

Going on pilgrimage to Mecca is one of the five pillars of Islam; it is the duty of Muslims to make the Hajj, the pilgrimage, at least once in their lifetime. It is a community event with each day's activities being mapped out by ancient custom and ritual. The command to go on Hajj is found in several places in the Qur'an.

You will need a picture of Mecca.

Key words
Hajj; Mecca; pilgrim.

Discussing the text
◆ Look at the picture of Mecca. What do the children know about Mecca and the pilgrimage? Look at the title and the opening paragraph of the extract to establish that this is an autobiographical account of first-hand experience.

◆ First reading: read though the text. What do the children learn about the author? Pose some questions which focus on the writer's feelings and attitude to being on Hajj, rather than on the detail of what happens. List any vocabulary that seems to capture some of those feelings.

◆ Encourage a discussion about the general content. How would the children feel going on Hajj?

◆ Second reading: read though the text again and draw out certain features from it.
Note the abbreviation p.b.u.h, short for Peace Be Upon Him, which Muslims say as a mark of respect to the Prophet. Remind the children that the reference is to the Prophet Muhammad.

◆ Look at the words, phrases and style which indicate that this is written from personal experience and is not a straightforward explanatory text.

◆ Look at the use of the word 'They' in 'They say that the first time'. To whom do the children think it refers?

◆ Identify what the writer presumes the reader will already know (for example, she makes no attempt to explain what Hajj is). Where does she offer an explanation to the reader?

◆ List the information about what happens on the Hajj that is contained in the text.

Further RE activities

◆ Research some topics on the Hajj, finding out the detail of what happens. Find out why it is so important to Muslims and discover where Mecca is.

◆ Look in reference books for examples and accounts of other pilgrimages across different religions, for example, Christian pilgrimages to Bethlehem and Jerusalem, and Hindu pilgrimages to Varanasi (Benares).

◆ Ask the children to talk about a journey that is important to them. Ask them to write about such a journey, concentrating on conveying their feelings when doing so.

◆ Discuss prayer and asking for wishes to come true. Why should you be careful about what you pray for? (You might also look at one or more of the wide number of stories where people have their wishes granted to their cost, for example, 'The Woodcutter and the Three Wishes', 'The Fisherman and the Flounder' or *Five Children and It* by E Nesbit.)

◆ Reflect on hierarchy and equality. How do people often try to indicate they think they are more important than others? In what ways can people be treated equally?

◆ Focus on commitment. How do people show their commitment to each other, and to God? What sort of things prompt such commitment?

Further literacy ideas

◆ Discuss words to do with status and hierarchy. Look for examples of hierarchies in society, for example 'general', 'colonel', 'captain'; 'headteacher', 'classteacher'.

◆ Look at the idea of saying 'They say'. Some examples can be proverbs, some can be hopes and others superstitions.

◆ Ask the children to compare this text with an account of the Hajj written in the third person from a textbook about religions. Look at the differences in style as well as content.

Why I Agree with Arranged Marriages

Genre
*non-fiction;
personal
reflection and
argument;
expository
text*

With any discussion on arranged marriages, the first thing you've got to clarify is the distinction between arranged and forced marriages. I totally disagree with any form of forced marriage. It is not only socially and Islamically unacceptable but, furthermore, results in pain and problems within a marriage set-up.

However, arranged marriage – the introduction of two suitable marital partners by a family member – proves not only to be statistically positive but also more prosperous. Arranged marriages leave the final say to the two individuals involved. This is the main reason why I agree with this way of finding a partner. After all, any relationship begins with an introduction. The relationship has to be initiated somehow, whether it's done by a friend, colleague or someone else. In the same way, within the Muslim community, the parents do the honours. This is a well set-up, good arrangement if done properly, not at all like Western conceptions of an arranged marriage.

I think even within Western society where most people find their own partner, the majority of parents will comment on their child's husband- or wife-to-be. In the Muslim community this is just more well-structured and arranged. However, even within the Muslim community, over the last couple of years, the trend of arranged marriage is

decreasing and being replaced by young people choosing their own partners. The direct result of this is a steadily increasing level of divorces.

I think because parents are older and wiser, and generally have their children's best interests at heart, they look for important qualities such as faith, character and stability. On the other hand looking for a suitor yourself has the danger of being misled by attraction, wealth, lust and such factors which often lead to marriage breakdown. It is always useful to have a third party opinion to ensure the right decision has been made, and parents can often pick up on signs of possible problems which their children might overlook because of being 'in love'. Allowing parents to help make the decision can avoid divorce in the long run.

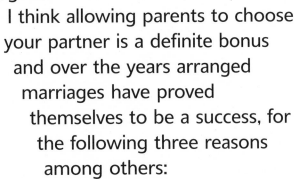

I think allowing parents to choose your partner is a definite bonus and over the years arranged marriages have proved themselves to be a success, for the following three reasons among others:

■ With arranged marriages parents provide ongoing support;

■ Parents will focus on compatibility rather than material qualities;

■ Because arranged marriages allow time to get to know the partner since they haven't met before, a couple works together as a closer network.

By Abeda Patel

Why I Agree with Arranged Marriages

TEACHERS' NOTES

Genre
non-fiction; personal reflection and argument; expository text

RE objective
◆ To develop understanding of Muslim ideas about the family.

Prior knowledge
None needed.

Background notes
This text is written by a Muslim student in her late teens. She has been brought up in England but intends to follow the custom of her faith and have an arranged marriage.

Forced marriages, where a girl is married against her will, are forbidden in Islam. The marriage ceremony involves the signing of a marriage contract during which the officiant asks the bride whether she consents to the marriage. Muslims often blame cultural factors and ignorance of the teaching of the Islamic faith for cases featured in the Western press, where a girl is tricked or forced into marriage. Some children will have some knowledge of arranged marriages from their own background.

Key words
Arranged marriage; community.

Discussing the text
◆ Look at the title and, if they don't already know, explain to the children what an arranged marriage is. How does it differ from their understanding of how people meet to get married?
◆ Read the first paragraph with the children, noting that the author presumes that her readers will know what a forced marriage is. What do the children think it is? Consider with them why the author might be anxious to distinguish between forced and arranged marriages.
◆ Have a dictionary on hand – some words may be unfamiliar to the children.
◆ Ask:: 'How do we find out the author's religious background? Does she tell us directly or indirectly?'
◆ Ask the children to list the author's arguments in favour of arranged marriages.
◆ Let the children discuss freely the views presented in the passage, without imposing your own.

Further RE activities
◆ Ask the children to research marriage practices in different religions.
◆ Discuss relationships with elders – and different ways of showing respect or disrespect.

Further literacy ideas
◆ Draw the children's attention to words and phrases which suggest that this is a persuasive text, presenting an argument, for example 'I totally disagree', 'However', 'After all' and 'On the other hand'.
◆ Ask the children to write definitions and/or synonyms for some of the key words and phrases, such as 'suitors', 'doing the honours', 'compatibility', 'stability' and 'bonus'.

Sikhism

Of all sacred texts, the Guru Granth Sahib is perhaps the one treated with the most reverence. Sikhs regard it as 'a living Guru', and its presence signifies the presence of God. It is a collection of hymns, some of which predate the first Sikh Guru, Guru Nanak who lived in the 15th century in North India. Most of the hymns, however, were written by Guru Nanak and several of the nine Gurus who succeeded him as leaders of the community. In 1649, the tenth Guru, Gobind Singh, declared the collection to be his successor. Decisions are made by at least five members of the Khalsa, the Sikh brotherhood, in the presence of the book. These hymns are both studied and sung in the gurdwara. We include one text from and one about the Guru Granth Sahib.

Sikhism, like all religions, has popular tales which are not regarded as sacred. Many of these are accounts of the lives of the Gurus, which stress their saintliness. These are known as janam (birth stories) and have been collected into several volumes. (The birth stories told here are in several different collections.)

The personal account of the religion ('Sunday Best', page 155) focuses on traditions also founded by Guru Nanak such as those of the community eating together and welcoming the needy and the stranger. Nanak spent years travelling as an itinerant minstrel and teacher, singing God's praises, overriding distinctions between religions and calling for a spirituality that belonged to the heart rather than the observation of empty ritual. On his return to his native region he established a town based on community – one in which jobs and food were shared among equals, in contrast with the hierarchical caste culture around them. Later, Sikhs were to permit some ritual within the faith, and they further emphasized the right to practise religious beliefs freely by calling on all Sikhs to fight for religious freedom.

A Hymn of Guru Nanak

from the Guru Granth Sahib

Genre
poetry; hymns

Thy praisers praise Thee
And know not thy greatness;
As rivers and streams flow into the sea,
But know not its vastness.

Kings who possess lands vast as the sea,
With wealth heaped high as the mountain,
Are not equal to the little worm
That forgets not God in its heart.

From the Sacred Writings of the Sikhs, translated by Dr Trilochan Singh, Bhai Jodh Singh,
Kapur Singh, Bawa Harkishen Singh, Khushwant Singh

A Hymn of Guru Nanak

Genre
Poetry; hymns

RE objective
To develop familiarity with Sikh texts.

Previous knowledge
Children need to have learned about Sikhism, including something about the Guru Granth Sahib.

Background notes
This text can be studied alongside the hymns of praise from Christianity (page 44) and Judaism (page 99); all three hymns link God with creation. Each one could be studied on a separate day in sequence. This Sikh text from the late 15th or early 16th century is one of the hymns in the Guru Granth Sahib.

Although all three hymns link God with creation, they each have a different focus. In the first verse of the Sikh hymn, the reference to nature is used as an analogy. Someone praising God has as little understanding of how great God really is as a river has any sense of how big the sea is. In the second verse, rather than God being compared to a king, there is a reminder that a king is nothing if he forgets God. There is also the idea that animals, even the lowly worm, can remember God; it is not just the prerogative of humans. It is usually sung with the accompaniment of a harmonium.

Key words
Praise; greatness.

Discussing the text
◆ Look at the title, or show the children a picture of the Guru Granth Sahib and/or Guru Nanak. Ask the children to recall what they know about them before introducing the text as a hymn from this sacred scripture.
◆ Read the whole hymn and ask for the children's initial thoughts, including whether it reminds them of anything else they have read. Then look through it, verse by verse.

◆ In saying God is great, what does the Guru mean – that God is literally physically bigger than everything else, or something different? What do the children think?

◆ Ask the children to imagine the river going into the sea. Wonder with them about whether the author really thinks the river understands anything at all. Why does the author use the picture of the river and the sea? What do they think he is trying to express or explain?

◆ Look at the contrast in the second verse – who do we usually think of as greater, the king or the worm? In the author's view, when is a king lower than a worm?

◆ Why do the children think Guru Nanak thinks remembering God is more important than anything?

◆ Read through the whole hymn again, perhaps listening to Sikh music while you do so.

Further RE activities

◆ Develop an understanding of the context of this hymn with further work on the Guru Granth Sahib (see page 150), and learn more about the gurdwara and the importance of singing and music in Sikh worship. You might look at the story of Guru Nanak and the robber (available in *A Tapestry of Tales*, see the Resources list, page 160) in which the robber is converted by the sound of Guru Nanak singing hymns.

◆ Compare this hymn with the hymns of praise from Christianity (see page 44) and Judaism (see page 99). Look specifically at the different ways the natural world is invoked in each.

◆ Discuss how music helps us to express our emotions, to calm our fears to cheer us up. Which music, songs or hymns have moved the children?

Further literacy ideas

◆ Look at some of the linguistic features of the hymn:
– the way a verb has been turned into a noun with 'praiser'. Point out that this is not a common form, and is probably not in the dictionary. Why would the translator have made it up? Make a list and experiment with verbs turned into agent nouns with the suffix '-er'. Encourage the children to check the words in dictionary to see if they are accepted in general usage. Try, for example, 'write', 'speak', 'hope', 'run', 'study', 'belief', 'teach', 'shop', 'weave', 'buy', 'sing' and 'eat'.
– the use of similes (for example 'lands as vast as the sea'). Ask the children to suggest other similes for 'large', such as 'her love was as great as…' and 'his bank balance was as large as…'.

◆ Ask the children to write a eulogy of praise (to God or a friend) based on comparatives. For example 'You are more beautiful than all the roses in world. My love is greater than all the stars in the sky.'.

The Guru Granth Sahib

Genre
non-fiction;
information
text
(explanatory
text)

If you go into a Sikh gurdwara you will be made very welcome. Sikhs like people to come in and join them, whether or not they are Sikhs themselves. But before you go into the main prayer room, you will be asked to make certain preparations, and you will see others doing the same. The reason for this is that when you go in, you will be in the presence of the Sikhs' most honoured teacher, guide and leader: their Holy Book, the Guru Granth Sahib.

Although the Guru Granth Sahib is a book, Sikhs believe that its words really are a living Guru (wise teacher) and they treat it as they would treat someone very important. They make sure that they are clean when they are in its presence. There are washbasins outside the prayer room in a gurdwara so that people can wash their hands before they go in. To show respect, they take off their shoes and they make sure their heads are covered. When people go into the prayer room, the first thing they do is approach the Guru Granth Sahib and kneel respectfully, as they put their gifts in front of it. They might bring money or some food to help make the meal after the service.

You have to go back 500 years to the end of the 1400s when the Sikh religion began to understand why Sikhs treat their Holy Book as a living teacher. Guru Nanak was the first teacher and leader of the Sikhs. As he travelled round India and other countries, he sang songs about God and about the way to live. People wrote down the words of these songs, as they were such beautiful poetry and they helped people to remember God. When Guru Nanak became old, he chose another man to be the Sikh Guru, to teach and guide people. When this Guru drew close to death, he chose the next Guru.

Each Guru in turn chose the one to follow him. All these men were wise and holy. It seemed that they loved God so much that they could not help singing his praises and writing poetry to help other people love him too. Sikhs believe that the poetry they wrote was the word of God.

In 1603 the fifth Guru, Guru Arjan, decided that all the poems written by the Gurus up to that time should be collected into one book. He sent messengers all over India, even as far as Sri Lanka, to ask people if they had written down any of the poems or hymns sung by the Gurus. One Sikh had a very large collection of the poems of Guru Ram Das, the fourth Guru. But he felt that it was too precious to lend to anyone. He would not give it to Guru Arjan's messenger. Eventually Guru Arjan went himself and persuaded the man to let him take it to be copied. The collection was carried in a great procession towards the town of Amritsar. When they came near, Guru Arjan's son came out to greet the arrival of the holy words.

Guru Arjan had a quiet room built where he would not be disturbed, and chose a faithful Sikh, Bhai Gurdas, to help him. They set to work to decide what should go in the book, and to arrange the hymns in a logical order. They put in thousands of hymns by the Gurus, including by Guru Arjan himself. They also decided to include poems by other holy people. It did not matter to Guru Arjan that they were not all Sikhs. If he found a poem which he felt spoke the truth about God, he included it in the book. So there are poems by Muslims and Hindus in the Guru Granth Sahib.

The work was finished in 1604 and become known as the Holy Granth. Granth means book. It was placed in the Golden Temple in Amritsar with great respect and much rejoicing. Now Sikhs could be sure that their hymns and teachings were not being altered by those who repeated them, and people would travel for miles to hear the book being read aloud.

Guru Arjan was eventually killed by the rulers of that part of India, because he would not give up his Sikh faith. When news of his death reached Amritsar, the Sikhs were full of sorrow. They showed their love for the Guru by reading aloud from the Holy Granth for ten days. Hearing the hymns encouraged Sikhs to continue their faith even though they were in danger.

About a hundred years later, Guru Gobind Singh, the tenth Guru, felt that the poems and hymns of his father, Guru Tegh Bahadur, should also be included in the collection. He decided where in the book they should go, and he dictated the whole book again while someone wrote it down, putting in Guru Tegh Bahadur's words where he wanted them to go.

Some of the Sikhs said to him, "You yourself have written many beautiful hymns which help us in our faith. Please put them in the Holy Granth, too." But Guru Gobind Singh was too modest to put his own words alongside those of the Gurus who had come before him.

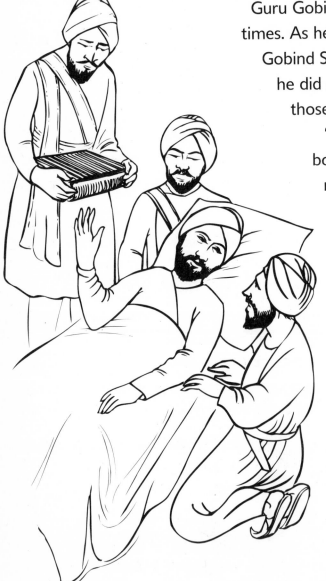

Guru Gobind Singh guided the Sikhs through difficult times. As he lay dying, the Sikhs wondered who Guru Gobind Singh would choose to be the next Guru. But he did not choose another man. Instead he said to those around him:

"Recognize the Holy Granth as the visible body of the Guru. The Sikh who wishes to meet me should find me in its words."

The Guru had chosen the Holy Granth to be the Sikh Guru for all time to come. From that time on, Sikhs have looked to the Holy Granth to be their guide and teacher in everything they do. They call it the Guru Granth Sahib, because Guru Gobind Singh told them that the Granth is now their Guru, and they add the word 'Sahib' which is used in India to speak about someone who is greatly respected.

The Guru Granth Sahib

Genre
*non-fiction;
information
text
(explanatory
text)*

RE objectives

◆ To learn strategies for extracting information from a text about a religion.

◆ To develop knowledge and understanding of the Sikh scriptures.

Prior knowledge

An introduction to Sikhism would be useful.

Background notes

This text could be used to expand the children's understanding having encountered the Guru Granth Sahib when learning about the gurdwara or Sacred Books.

Key words

Guru Granth Sahib; Sikh.

Discussing the text

◆ Look at the heading. Note that it is not in English, but in Panjabi. Ask the children what they know already about the Guru Granth Sahib. Perhaps look at a picture.

◆ After each paragraph has been read, ask each child to think of one thing they have learned from the paragraph, then pool some of the statements.

◆ Check that the children understand that the Guru was not only the teacher but also the leader of the Sikh community, and that each dying Guru named a leader to succeed him. Make a timeline of the history of the Guru Granth Sahib picking out key people and events, beginning with Guru Nanak and ending with Guru Gobind Singh. (You may not be able to put a date to every event but you will be able to establish a chronology.)

◆ Ask the children what the hymns and poems were about – pick out the key phrases in the text which say something about the poems themselves.

◆ Discuss the attitude of Sikhs to the Guru Granth Sahib, how they show it respect and why it is important to them.

◆ Check whether they understand that the Guru Granth Sahib is a collection of hymns written by the Sikh Gurus and other writers and gathered over a number of years.

◆ Make a glossary from the text of key Sikh words. (Use only information from the text.)

◆ Ask the children to write a heading for each paragraph. Then ask them to make a list of questions, the answers to which can be found in the text. For example 'What do Sikhs do when they go into the prayer room?' Children might swap questions and then write the answers.

◆ Discuss for whom the piece is written. Does the writer think the readers will be Sikhs or non-Sikhs?

Further RE activities

◆ Develop understanding of the Guru Granth Sahib further by listening to a recording of the Guru Granth Sahib being sung. This is available with *A Gift to the Child* (see the Resources list, page 160). You might also read and perhaps make a collection of other stories about the Sikh Gurus, especially Guru Nanak and Guru Gobind Singh. You might read a translation of a hymn found in the Guru Granth Sahib, for example on page 147 of this book or you could visit a gurdwara.

◆ Put the Guru Granth Sahib into historical context by making a timeline. Ask the children to carry out some research using reference books so that they can put the dates of the first and last Sikh Gurus on a timeline with other religious leaders, such as Jesus and the Prophet Muhammad. Add some key events or rulers in British and Indian history to the timeline made when reading the text.

◆ Look at similarities and differences between the treatment of the Guru Granth Sahib and other holy writings.

◆ Discuss the link between leadership and teacher. Why do the children think the Sikh leaders were also called teachers? In what ways are teachers today leaders, and in what ways are leaders teachers?

Further literacy ideas

◆ Look for linguistic features in the text:

– words or phrases associated with time to show the date, or to indicate its passing. What other words or phrases can be used to indicate a date, or to show that time has moved on?

– make a list of titles which go with respected positions in English.

– choose one sentence from the text, for example, 'Guru Arjan had a quiet room built where he would not be disturbed and chose a faithful Sikh, Bhai Gurdas, to help him.' Ask the children to take away one or more words at a time, the rule being that a sentence must still remain and it must make some sense. Then discuss why the author has included the words that were taken away. What meaning did they add to the sentence? The children could also write a series of sentences, each containing three words only, to convey the same meaning.

◆ Look for examples of other anthologies of poetry and hymns. Look in their introductions for information on how they were collected.

◆ Encourage the children to begin their own private collection of poems, writings or hymns that are important to them.

Genre
non-fiction;
information
text/
newspaper
reports

Sunday Best

Big family meals may be a thing of the past for many Britons. But not for the nation's Sikhs, who swell the temples in their thousands to break bread and share prayers.

As Britain in the 21st century becomes a snacking society, there is one community for whom the traditional ritual of eating together is still sacred. And even increasingly popular. But not for them the Sunday roast that was the peak of the week's eating. Because the biggest Sunday dinner served in Britain today is the communal Sikh meal known as langar.

Go to any of Britain's 200-odd Sikh temples (gurdwaras) and at most times of the day you will find food on offer. And on Sunday evenings, the traditional time for Britain's 300 000 Sikhs to gather for worship, there can be a feeding of the five thousand in the largest gurdwaras. Literally. Catering for such numbers sounds a difficult and daunting task. But, remarkably, every week, in each gurdwara, a different family takes on the job.

Shepherd's Bush in West London has Britain's oldest gurdwara. On a Sunday morning, the Bhasin family are already hard at work in the gurdwara's kitchen. Red kidney beans have been soaking in washing-up bowls overnight, ready to be turned into moti – an almost chewy bean curry – and freshly pressed paneer (curd cheese), sharpened with a squirt of lemon juice, is resting like rising dough in basins.

"Why we're doing the langar today," says the mother of the family, Baljit Kaur, as she starts to chop the first of a sackload of onions in the communal kitchen, while husband Jaswant takes a cup of sugary temple tea, "is to celebrate our Silver Wedding." Family elders have flown in from India, and nephews and nieces have come down from Newcastle for the occasion. But the most practised helpers are the couple's daughters: Inderjeet and her younger sister, Dilpreet.

Service, or seva, is a sacred duty for Sikhs – which comes in handy when it comes to onion-chopping or doing the washing-up. But then, Sikhism – which was founded by Guru Nanak only five centuries ago – is a deeply practical religion in most matters. Especially when it comes to food. "Guru Ji taught that there should always be food at the temple," says Inderjeet, a student, as she deseeds the red chillies that will later be stirred in with the onion and spices to make a masala sauce. "He said that if followers had come to the temple from far away, then they had to eat. You can't learn on an empty stomach."

But it is also very important that everyone sits down to eat together. Nanak taught that everyone was equal, so everyone in the gurdwara should eat together, whatever background, status or sex. The food can be prepared by anyone and served by anyone. There's total equality. When the great Emperor Akbar travelled to meet Guru Amar Das, one of Nanak's successors, the Guru refused to see him until he had sat on the floor and eaten with other followers.

And so it is today. As Sunday morning unwinds into Sunday afternoon, everyone in the family – young and old, men and women – pitches into the cooking. "It's a big thing for us," says Inderjeet, as she supervises the spinach. "Langar helps bind the community together." And it seems so, as ever-increasing numbers of cousins, aunts, uncles and family friends join in. Everywhere in the Shepherd's Bush kitchen, there's chopping, slicing, stirring and frying going on. With 500 evening meals to make, it's cooking on an industrial scale.

While each family that takes on the weekly cook-in has its own variations on the theme, gurdwara food is always simple rather than showy. And the meal is vegetarian so that everyone can eat together. Most weeks, there is a consistent combination of dishes on the menu: usually something moist – often daal – plus a dry dish such as spinach and curd cheese (sag paneer). To help mop up the juices of the dishes on offer, there's also the bread to be made. And lots of it.

The Bhasin's sweet for the day – and one that needs constant stirring – is semya, which looks a bit like cut-up spaghetti when it's dry but, once

cooked with milk and bagloads of sugar, swells and fattens into something a bit like a sickly semolina.

While the Bhasin family finishes cooking the main meal, over on the other side of the kitchen an impressively muscle-bound priest – who looks as if he could be an expert in Sikh wrestling – is stirring semolina into sugar syrup to make Kara Prashad: the Holy Sweet that is handed out at Sikh services and that symbolizes the goodness of God. As he stirs and works, his lips move in silent prayer with the rhythm.

Upstairs, in the main prayer-hall, the faithful are already gathering. Shedding their shoes as they come in, they bow down before the Guru Granth Sahib, the Sikh scriptures that are regarded as the last and living guru. Downstairs, in the kitchen, loudspeakers carry the drone of harmonium music and the sound of the opening evening prayers to the cooks, and speed them into a final flurry of culinary activity. Old men in turbans, young women in vivid kameez tops and matching scarves, children with their hair tucked in buns, all help with the finishing touches, while a chain of mothers kneads, flours, rolls, grills, flips and plates a stack of chapatis.

As the Ardas, Sikhism's central prayer, begins to ascend to its climax, Jaswant and Baljit slip out of the kitchen with a tray of the finished food – roti, sag paneer, semya, salad, yoghurt, chapatis. The couple bow before the Scriptures and then offer the food for blessing, because that which has been given by the Guru must first be given to him.

With the food blessed, the communal eating can begin. Sitting as equals on the floor, the 500 faithful meet, greet, chat and tuck-in. And in the kitchen there is a collective sigh of relief. "Normally, you would be nervous doing this sort of thing," says Baljit with a smile. "You'd worry if the food would be cooked, if there will be enough. But in the temple it is always cooked and there is always enough. Everything seems to happen of its own accord. It's almost supernatural." If only the same applied to the washing-up.

By Nigel Duckers from The Guardian Weekend, 8 Jan 2000, slightly adapted.

Sunday Best

RE objectives

◆ To develop knowledge of
the Sikh langar.

Prior knowledge

Some background knowledge of Sikhism would be desirable, though the newspaper article will probably have been read by people with no such knowledge. From the literacy point of view it is preferable if you do not have to fill in any gaps in the children's knowledge since they are learning to read with knowledge they already have at their disposal.

Equality is a key concept in the teaching of Sikhism, demonstrated practically in the gurdwara, where the idea is that everyone is on an equal footing.

Key words

Langar; gurdwara; equality; seva.

Discussing the text

◆ First focus on the activity in the text: read through the first paragraph. Briefly pool or make connections with any prior knowledge or experience of Sikhism. Wonder with the children about the connection between the title and Sikhs (see the notes on 'wondering' in the Introduction, page 6).

◆ Read the next two paragraphs and clarify even further what this article is going to be about. Where are the events taking place?

◆ Ask the children to try and picture the changing scenes in their heads as you read the rest of the article to them. Then, on completing the reading, encourage the children to describe what they have imaged, finding words to describe the atmosphere. Is it quiet and peaceful or busy? What sort of food is being cooked?

◆ Look at the people in the account. What are they doing? Finish the sentences with the children:

Baljit Kaur is…

Jaswant is…

Inderjeet is…

◆ Discuss why they think the writer called the article 'Sunday Best'.

◆ Do the children think the writer is a Sikh himself? If not, why not? What is his attitude towards Sikhs? For example, is he critical of them, does he find them interesting, does he like the atmosphere?

◆ Discuss why vegetarian food is served in the langar.

◆ Re-read the text to learn more about Sikhism: make a list with the children of things that we learn about Sikhism, its teachers, its worship and its holy book from the text.

◆ Ask the children to skim read to see which food is special to the Sikh religion.

◆ What indicates that Sikhism has links with India?

◆ Is there anything in the report that surprised or interested the children? Make a list of questions prompted by the text and discuss where you would go to find an answer.

◆ Discuss the children's ideas of equality. How does the account show that Sikhism teaches equality?

Further RE activites

◆ Develop the children's understanding of the gurdwara and follow through questions raised by the text. You might put the questions on a noticeboard and children can fill in answers as they find them. Read and find out more about the Sikh Gurus. You might read and discuss the story of Guru Amar Das and Emperor Akbar in *REAL Infant Assembly Book* (see the Resources list, page 160). Read the story of the writing of the Guru Granth Sahib, page 150. Make a model of a gurdwara from two shoeboxes, with the prayer hall and the kitchen. Help the children to make small figures to go inside.

◆ Develop the children's understanding of Sikhism as a religion originating in India by discussing that Sikh food is Indian food, noting that Sikhism is one religion of India and that people from other religions in the Indian sub-continent also eat these sorts of food. Have a tasting session of some of these foods which, while not strictly speaking religious education, will make it all come alive. Look at the role of food in religious ritual.

◆ Find out about other ceremonies in which food is blessed, for example the Jewish Sabbath, Hindu prasad, Christian Communion service and saying graces or blessings before meals. Discuss food and special occasions and the idea of hospitality. Encourage the children to talk about any special meals they have experienced. Discuss the symbolism of sweet food. Why do they think it is used as a symbol for the goodness of God?

◆ Follow through the theme of equality. Discuss what it means to treat everybody as equals.

Further literacy ideas

◆ Look at the linguistic features of the text:

– make a list of all the words to do with eating in the text, including but not confined to the names of food.

– look at what is said in speech marks. Who is the speaker talking to? (Clearly the author – the speech in the account is not conversation between people). Turn the direct speech into indirect speech and compare it. Why do the children think the writer used direct speech?

◆ Discuss whether this article is news although it comes from a newspaper. Look at weekend magazines. How are they different from the rest of the newspaper? Why do they come with the newspaper at the weekend?

◆ Ask the children to pretend to be a reporter visiting a regular communal event. Encourage them to write an article about it in which they try to convey the atmosphere, the attitudes and the reasons for certain activities. This could be a communal meal (for example, school dinner), a family ritual, or another ritual such as a football match.

Resources

◆ *The Barefoot Book of Buddhist Tales*, by Sherab Chodzin and Alexandra Kohn (Barefoot Books).

◆ *Collected Poems of Longfellow* on the Internet: http://www.auburn.edu/~vestmon/longfellow.html

◆ *A Gift to the Child: Religious Education in the Primary School*, ed. Michael Grimmett et al. (Simon and Schuster Education). Contains a useful list of books and resources.

◆ *100 Ideas for RE*, by Sandra Palmer and Elizabeth Breuilly (Collins Educational).

◆ *Jataka Tales*: There are several children's versions of Jataka stories currently in print. Two possible sources are:

Clearvision Trust
tel: 0161 839 9579, fax: 0161 839 4815 e-mail: clearvision@clear-vision.org
Dharma publishing through Windhorse Publications
e-mail: windhorse@compuserve.com,
11 Park Road, Moseley, Birmingham, B13 8AB, Tel/fax: +44 (0) 121 449 9191

◆ *The Ramayana, A Journey*, by Ranchor Prime (Collins and Brown) is no longer in print. However the following copies are readily available and suitable for younger readers:
The Ramayana, by R K Narayan (Penguin).
The Ramayana, by Krishna Dharma (Torchlight Publishing).

◆ *REAL Infant Assembly Book*, by Sandra Palmer and Elizabeth Breuilly (Collins Educational)

◆ *REAL Junior Teachers' Handbook*, by Sandra Palmer and Elizabeth Breuilly (Collins Educational)

◆ Several versions of the story of St Gerasimus and the lion are available on the Internet (search for 'Saint Gerasimus'). It can also be found in *Beasts and Saints*, edited by Helen Waddell, (Darton, Longman & Todd).

◆ *Stories from the Jewish World*, by Sybil Sheridan (Macdonald Young Books).

◆ *Stories from the Christian World*, by David Self (Macdonald Young Books).

◆ *A Tapestry of Tales*, by Sandra Palmer and Elizabeth Breuilly (Collins Educational).